Y

our children are not your children.

They are the sons and daughters of Life's longing for itself

They come through you but not from you,

And though they are with you yet they belong not to you.

You may give them your love but not your thoughts,

For they have their own thoughts.

You may house their bodies but not their souls,

For their souls dwell in the house of tomorrow,

which you cannot visit, not even in your dreams.

—FROM THE PROPHET, BY KAHLIL GIBRAN

DIG/U.S.A.

is an exciting new source book of the most relevant contemporary materials: from newspapers, novels, songs and films to statistics, cartoons, photographs and advertisements.

Focusing on the issues that deeply concern today's youth, it provides a unique approach to critical thought and creative response, with projects for discussion, writing and research.

Speak out on: The Generation Gap • Family Problems • Youth Culture • The New Morality • Drugs • Crime • Dissent and Conformity.

4/26/04

To Bert

From Jane

No matter how things change, things still stay the³ same.

$$\text{RLI: } \frac{\text{VLM } 7.0}{\text{IL } 8\text{--}12}$$

DIG/U.S.A.
A Bantam Pathfinder edition/published December 1970
2nd printing

To The Reader

If you are a young American, this book is about you, and for you. It is about your music, your clothes, your friends and families, your ideas about life and society, your differences with parents, teachers, and others in authority.

Much of it was written by people with strong opinions who wanted to convince others of their viewpoint. But the book itself takes no sides. Different readers might find the same item enjoyable or maddening; they might wish to challenge or support it. The book is meant to stir you to action: thinking-action, talking-action, feeling-action, doing-action. It is meant to help you hammer out your personal position on events and problems that affect everyone.

We hope you will add to the book as you find new evidence in daily life, evidence needed to tell the whole story. Only your individual choices and judgments can give the book its final shape.

The Editors

Look, your father and I don't ask for very much. We're only interested in your happiness. Please—finish school.

But Ma, the stuff in school is just not my bag—and besides, it's my life, and I have to find out how to live it.

1.
This
Generation

CBS

MRS. HOLMES:

They're just frustrated, I guess. I really don't know. They have every material thing they could have. And this is what their parents thought they wanted. And yet they say now they hate their parents, and their parents were wrong, so . . . I don't know what those kids want.

MRS. FLEMING:

She sort of systematically attacks everything I hold near and dear and sacred. Like, you name it — God, the flag, the king. She can't discuss religion, politics, sex, or drugs with me. You know, is there anything else? Like the weather, you know . . .

MR. McGRAW:

Because they have lived under different circumstances, always at war, always problems in the cities, always problems in the rural areas of America, they are worried. They have taken the burdens and the problems of America prematurely upon their shoulders, something that my generation didn't do.

CBS REPORTS: GENERATIONS APART, as broadcast over the CBS Television Network

CBS

TEX HOLMES:

I think there's a large generation gap today. And I don't really think it's being exaggerated very much. Because there are an awful lot of kids who just can't talk to their parents. They can't talk about anything. Their parents just kind of shut them off and the kids, on the other hand, do the same thing. And so it's a real problem of communications.

NITA FLEMING:
I think the degree of difference is such that my parents will probably never really understand what I think about a lot of things, never really understand me or know me. I think it's gone almost beyond that.

PAT McGRAW:
It seems to me that the generation before this one, and my father in particular, were very expedient. You know, what's the best way to do it? There was no question, for example, in my father's mind, that he ought to join the army. Well, there's a very big question in my mind.

11

The Generation Gap

"Telling it like it is" was in the fashion long enough to become a boring cliche, and even when it was fresh it had a subjective quality that undermined its usefulness.

"Telling it like it is," of course, depends on who is doing the telling.

There for a time, the tellers generally were assumed to be under 30, pure of spirit and direct in thought and speech.

But there are no age limits for telling it like it is. Every generation has its blunt speakers who have no compunctions about dishing up the plain truth as they see it.

One of the bluntest speeches of this nature that we have come across in a long time was given by Prof. Lawrence Lee to members of a social fraternity at the University of Pittsburgh:

"You have been told, and you have come to believe, that you are the brightest of generations ... You are, rather, one of the most self-centered, self-pitying generations.

"The generation gap is one of the delusions of your generation — and to some men of my generation. . . .

"The only generation gap is that we have lived longer, we know more than you do from having lived, and we are so far ahead of you that it will take you a lifetime to have the same relative knowledge and wisdom.

"You had better learn from us while you can. . . .

"It is not mawkish to love one's country.

"The country, with all of its agony and all of its faults, is still the most generous and the most open society on the earth. . . .

"All generations need the help of all others. Ours is asking yours to be men rather than children, before some tyrant with the aid of other frightened and ignorant men seeks to make all of us slaves in reaction to your irresponsibility."

And that is telling it the way it is, or at least the way it seems to Lawrence Lee of the University of Pittsburgh.

I think it is fair to describe yours as a generation of unusually genuine and intense concern with social justice and intellectual freedom.
—J. F. Kennedy

CBS

CHIP WILLIAMS: They've kind of lost what life's about. They—they live their own lives, they go to work from eight to four, and they come home, and they just sit and talk and watch TV. I don't know, I think they've really kind of lost, in many cases, a feeling for life, what it is.

LYNN AARONS: They forgot how to be young, I guess. They've grown old, and they get so tied up, you know, they just get so tied up that they can't enjoy things.

```
SONNY FLOWERS: They're inflexible,
they're proud, they're arrogant,
they're sure they have the right way,
you know. And they're scared. That—that
fear thing is probably the biggest
thing.
```

NITA McWATTERS: And perhaps they've grown a little bit too closed-minded too. Where they're comfortable, they don't want somebody else coming in and making them uncomfortable. Therefore they don't want to hear the things that are going to make them uncomfortable.

1 ASKED OF PARENTS: What is it about the younger generation that bothers you the most? (FREE RESPONSE)

	Total Parents	Parents College Youth	Parents Non-college Youth
Grooming and appearance	21%	14%	23%
No respect for authority or their elders	20	17	20
Nothing—the majority are good kids	14	16	13
Self-centered and lack of responsibility	11	10	12
Immature and naive	11	11	11
Rebellious—want too much freedom	10	8	10
Use drugs and LSD	11	9	12

2 ASKED OF YOUTH: Would you please complete the following sentence for me. The main trouble with the young generation is: (FREE RESPONSE)

	Total Youth	College	Non-college
Immature and naive	21%	25%	20%
Too impatient	13	16	12
Intolerant and close-minded	10	12	10
No respect for authority or parents	10	7	11
Self-centered and lack of responsibility	10	8	11
Doesn't try to communicate with older people	10	11	10
Has too much freedom	9	4	10
Nothing—there is no trouble	9	9	9

Survey conducted for CBS NEWS by Daniel Yankelovich, Inc.

CBS REPORTS: GENERATIONS APART, as broadcast over the CBS Television Network

DIALOG

Look, your father and I don't ask for very much. We're only interested in your happiness. Please—finish school.

But Ma, the stuff in school is just not my bag—and besides, it's my life, and I have to find out how to live it.

What do you mean I should be grateful for all you've given me? All you've given me is a world about to fall apart.

If I catch you running around with any more of those hairy, doped up freaks, you've had it.

▶ _____
_____
_____
_____

▶ _____
_____
_____
_____

16

17

INTERVIEWER:
And what is there about the generation gap that bothers you the most?

WOMAN:
I think the complete lack of respect for authority. We always, when I was a girl, we were taught to respect our elders.

Every man over forty is a scoundrel.

—G. B. Shaw

MY GENERATION

People try to put us down
Just because we get around.
Things they do look awful cold
Hope I die before I get old.

This is my generation, baby.

Why don't you all f-f-f-fade away
Don't try and dig what we all say
I'm not trying to cause a big sensation
I'm just talking 'bout my generation.

This is my generation, baby,
My generation.

**—Peter Townshend
(for the Who)**

the small society

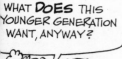

WHAT **DOES** THIS YOUNGER GENERATION WANT, ANYWAY?

THEY'RE LOOKING FOR ANSWERS—

ANSWERS? ANSWERS TO WHAT?

Congressional Record—Senate

FEBRUARY 25, 1969

INVOLVEMENT OF YOUTH
(By Edward M. Kennedy, Senator from Massachusetts)

On a mild spring evening in Indianapolis, during the primary election campaign this year, 22 young Americans sat down to talk.

After riding many hours in buses and sleeping on benches in campaign headquarters, they had spent a grueling Saturday on the sidewalks of the city taking the issues to the people. Now it was time to take stock.

They talked of Republicans who refused to hear them out, of Democrats who would not budge on Vietnam, of black children flocking to pass out campaign buttons, of whites in streets as grubby as any Negro ghetto showing quiet pleasure that an educated visitor wanted to hear what they thought.

The canvassers for Robert Kennedy that I met with that night were engaged in the kind of active political work by young people that characterized this year's primary elections. When they started that morning they had been novices. The next morning they would return to the sidewalks older by more than a day.

At about the same time last spring, another group of young people was pursuing a different course at Columbia University. The issues they held up to the university—construction of a college gymnasium in a Negro neighborhood, Columbia's affiliation with a Defense Department research organization—reflected beneath their surface real questions about the right of students to a share in the governing of their school.

The Columbia protest added up to the occupation of five campus buildings, the ransacking of administrative offices, and a bloody confrontation with police with more than 100 seriously injured and nearly 700 arrests.

It would be comfortable to conclude that the young folks in Indiana were working responsibly within the established system while those at Columbia were working irresponsibly against it.

It is more important to realize that both were working for what they

by BRICKMAN

IF THEY WANT THE **RIGHT** ANSWERS WHY DON'T THEY COME TO US?

THEY **DID** COME TO US—

BUT THEY HAD THE WRONG QUESTIONS—

Washington Star Syndicate, Inc.   BRICKMAN   9-

believed in. One group hoped positive efforts would be effective; the other had concluded that they wouldn't.

The distance between confidence and futility is growing small with American youth today. Some believe our society will always work, and some believe it will never work again. Most, I suspect, are in the middle.

Today's young people don't share the historic guideposts of their elders. They did not know the mobilization of resources and patriotism brought on by the two world wars. They did not feel the comradeship of disaster created by the Great Depression. They were too young to grasp the national fear of global communism in the early 1950s.

They are spared the emotions of the past. They come to us with fresh vision. And with all the right questions.

They want to know why the war to preserve the freedom of South Vietnam kills or injures more than 200,000 civilians of that country each year.

They want to know why, with the United Nations more than 23 years old, the world is stockpiling nuclear weapons, enough to destroy civilization several times over.

They want to know why Negroes can fight in America's wars but often can't live in America's suburban neighborhoods.

They want to know why, in the wealthiest and most highly educated society in history, the poor are expected to break out of the ghettoes with no money and no education.

The young are told, "It's much better than it used to be." And they reply, "But why is it still as bad as it is?"

They are not only asking disturbing questions. They are also suggesting to America that the legacy they will inherit is worth saving, but not by much.

To say that the younger generation is going to the dogs is not only foolish but futile. For one thing, whatever the young choose to be is a reflection of what their elders have taught them to be, by direction or by neglect. For another, writing off the young is like saying that our nation will come to a noble but sad end in 30 or 40 years.

The way to appeal to the young is not to deplore them, but to put faith in them. The Peace Corps put faith in them, and they responded. VISTA put faith in them and they responded. The Teacher Corps put faith in them, and they responded.

For there is no question that the young people of today are a remarkable generation.

21

...AND THEY SHALL COVER

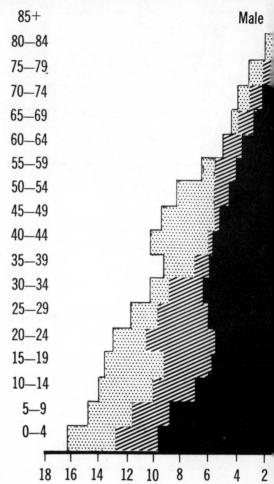

Male

Age
85+
80—84
75—79
70—74
65—69
60—64
55—59
50—54
45—49
40—44
35—39
30—34
25—29
20—24
15—19
10—14
5—9
0—4

18 16 14 12 10 8 6 4 2

Population (millions)

Projected Year
1955
1980
2000

Source: Population Reference Bureau, Inc., Washington 36, D.C., U.S. Population Growth, 1960-2000, February 1964.

THE FACE OF THE EARTH.

—Exodus 10, 5

Female

AGE PROFILE OF
U.S. POPULATION,
1955, 1980, AND 2000

2   4   6   8   10   12   14   16

U.S. TOTAL POPULATION BY AGE GROUPS

	1960		2000	
All Ages ...	100.0%	179,323,000	100.0%	349,215,000
Under 14 ..	29.6%	53,048,000	29.4%	102,832,000
14-65	61.2%	109,715,000	61.6%	214,998,000
65 and Over	9.2%	16,560,000	9.0%	31,385,000

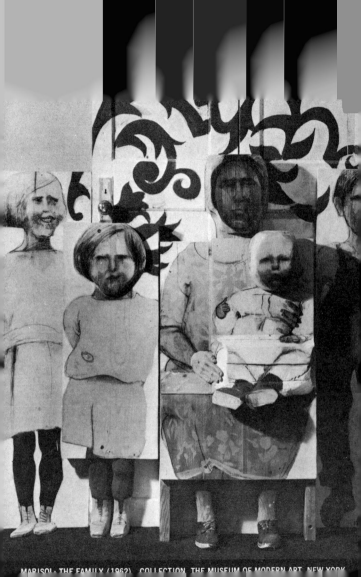

MARISOL. THE FAMILY (1962). COLLECTION, THE MUSEUM OF MODERN ART, NEW YORK

*"If it weren't for four younger
kids in the family I'd walk
out of here tomorrow."*

2.
The Family

Ann Landers

First Things First: Go Back to School

By ANN LANDERS

DEAR ANN LANDERS: I am a girl, 17, and my life is a nightmare. If it weren't for four younger kids in the family I'd walk out of here tomorrow.

Dad is drunk every night of his life. Mom has had a nervous breakdown and is very forgetful. My 14-year-old sister and I do the housework, washing, ironing and cooking because Mom is always in bed with terrible headaches. Dad says her illnesses are phony and that her lousy disposition has driven him to drink. Mom says his drinking has ruined her life and made her sick.

I quit school last fall because Dad lost his job and his unemployment compensation wasn't enough to feed and clothe us. I feel as though I'm cracking up. Please tell me what to do.

ALICE

DEAR ALICE: The first thing you should do is get back in school. The few dollars you are making aren't worth the sacrifice. Next call Family Service. They will send a caseworker out to evaluate the situation and provide help and guidance.

It doesn't matter whether your dad drinks because your mother has a lousy disposition or your mother has a lousy disposition because your dad drinks. The important thing is that they both get help so you and your brothers and sisters can have a decent life.

Village Bulletin Board

SAM S. R. Please write or call collect. Haven't heard from you for over a month now. Ma & Pa.

JUSTIN
for the love of God come back. We feel terrible. Be merciful to us. You won't have any problems we can't solve.

CATHY, CALL MOM. SHE IS VERY, VERY ILL OR CALL ME OR CHARLOTTE—JOYCE

SHERRI LYN
Pumpkin! I'm home. Why aren't you! Love Mother

SHARON—PLEASE COME HOME. WE LOVE YOU AND WANT YOU BACK. MOM, DAD, D. AND K.

PAMELA—Remember Tony—Mama & Granny sick— Accident settled — We understand — Not Mad — Please write and call collect — Daddy

---

Tony—Please Contact—We miss you—Same address, same phone. Ronnie, Lynda and Leslie

Lost time, lost people, and lost love—forever lost!
—Thomas Wolfe

RATE PER 1,000 POPULATION

Source: Department of Health, Education, and Welfare, Office of Child Development

Divorce Rates

PERCENT INVOLVING CHILDREN

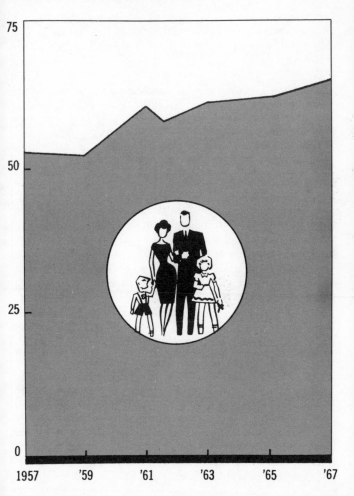

TWO BLOCKS APART

sends me up to the store for something, to get bread and milk or do some shopping. He might say, "And please get the *Times* when you come back." So sometimes I might bring the bread and milk and the other food and forget the *Times,* or else I bring home the wrong newspaper. That gets my father furious and he calls me a stupid idiot. He says that I'm very smart and that I should use my brains and not do things like that.

But my father has explained to us what he wants for us and how he wants to help us grow up right. One night he took me into his room and we had a long talk and he told me that when he was eleven years old he used to hang out in an old shack with his friends. It was a place that older kids used and sometimes, when the little boys were playing there, they'd hear these bigger boys planning to rob a grocery store or something like that. My father said "Peter, I was really brought up with hoodlums, really bad ones. I know that there's nothing like that in your life now, but I don't ever want you to get anywhere near that, because it's a terrible life." Because of the hard time he had, my father always tells me to keep up, to pay attention to etiquette, to my studies. My father went to college, but it wasn't easy for him the way it will be for me. He had to work his way through Notre Dame and then, after he graduated he got a good job. Now he's vice president of a very big and important company and really knows himself how to succeed and how to have a good life.

I don't understand this psychology or whatever it is. I don't understand that. Child psychology is no way to bring up children. You shouldn't do certain things because they're bad, and how is your boy going to understand? How are you going to teach a blind person what the color red looks like? I think that if I had a child, and he was playing with fire, I wouldn't tell him that it was bad in a quiet voice. You would really have to do something powerful to show him. Or else, I suppose, let him get burned. In a way, my father tries to protect us from getting burned by good discipline. Then the other side of this is that my father is always fair. I never resented even a spanking because whenever I got one, my parents were always sure that I needed it, that I'd really done something I needed to be straightened out about. I could see it myself.

stopped to think that they could—you know— hold on to you and give you a guide and show you how to swim.

Everybody down there was so much savage in a way. I am not trying to say that my family was savages. All I'm saying is that they didn't know how to act. They didn't communicate civilized. They didn't talk back and forth like other people do. They would fight, they would argue, and whoever was stronger would win. And that's who would rule in that family household or outside. If you couldn't handle yourself, even when you were real small, that was your tough luck.

But now it's different. Like my mother, you know, she's been through it. Before, she would yell all the time, yell and scream and hit us. But now, no fights, no arguments.

Like it's the atmosphere. I mean, you're not talking the way you were before because the past couple of years you don't have to fight against anybody else for your food. You can do it on your own. And this way, you feel more reliable, like to yourself and to others.

My mother even got to be a floor lady. She had studied from nothing, I mean, working on a sewing machine she didn't even know how to operate and now she can take a machine apart and put it back together and she knows all types of different machines. She was a floor lady for a long time, so now she knows that wherever she goes in New York, if anything goes wrong on us, she can always find a job. In Puerto Rico, what can she do?

And I think she's happier now. She can find—well—other people wouldn't, but what we would call the luxuries. And what can you get over there? Only mud and screaming and being beaten up.

You know, it is a funny thing about my family. My father wasn't ever really with us. Since I came to New York, my father has never been with us. My mother divorced him after we got here and that was it. He went his way and I went mine—we went ours. He was supposed to pay alimony and he was paying fifteen dollars I think. As the years grew, went by, he started to slow the payments and then didn't want to pay at all because we were getting a little older. And it stated right there that he had to pay until we were eighteen. My little

Remember when home was a place
where the whole family got together?
Go home this weekend.
Long Distance is the next best thing to being there.

MOTHER TO SON

Well, son, I'll tell you:
Life for me ain't been no crystal stair.
It's had tacks in it,
And splinters,
And boards torn up,
And places with no carpet on the floor—
Bare.
But all the time
I'se been a-climbin' on,
And reachin' landin's
And turnin' corners,
And sometimes goin' in the dark
Where there ain't been no light.
So, boy, don't you turn back.
Don't you set down on the steps
'Cause you finds it kinder hard.
Don't you fall now—
For I'se still goin', honey,
I'se still climbin',
And life for me ain't been no crystal stair.

—Langston Hughes

could have told them a whole lot of stuff that would have helped them, Mama and Dad and Papa, everybody, if they had only listened to me.

I remember how Dad thought being a busboy was a real good job. When I was working at Hamburger Heaven, I stayed there for a year, and I don't know how I did it. I was working for nine hours a day, six days a week, and going to school at night. He still felt that this was a good job, because he'd never made any money. He'd never made more than sixty dollars a week in his life until recently. I suppose when he was my age, he was only making something like thirty dollars a week and thought it was a whole lot of money. He figured if I was making forty-five dollars a week, that was a whole lot of money. The cat was crazy. I would spend forty-five dollars on a pair of shoes. To him it was a good job because when he was nine years old, he'd plowed the fields from sunup to sundown.

I came in one night and told Mama. I said, "Mama, I'm gon quit this job at Hamburger Heaven, because it's getting too damn hard on me."

Dad was sitting over in the corner in his favorite chair reading the newspaper. He wouldn't look up, because we could never talk. We just never talked too much after we had our last fight.

I said I was going to school, and that plus the job was kind of rough on me.

After Dad couldn't take any more, he lifted his head out of the paper and said, "Boy, you don't need all that education. You better keep that job, because that's a good job."

"Yeah, Dad, it's good as long as you can take it, but if it kills you, there's nothing good about that."

He said, "Hard work ain't never killed nobody, unless they was so lazy that thinkin' about it killed 'em."

I said, "I know one thing. It's not gon kill me now, because I already quit it."

He said, "Yeah, well, it sure seems funny to me, you quittin' your job, talkin' about you can't do that and go to school. You ought to stop goin' to school. You didn't want to go to school when I was sendin' you there. Your Mama would take you in one door and you'd sneak out the other door. Even the truant officer couldn't keep you in school. Boy, I think you're dreamin'. You better stop all that dreamin' and go out there and get yourself a good job and keep it while you got it."

I'M REALLY DRAGGED BUT NOTHING
GETS ME DOWN

Hershey took out another cigar. "And *your* boy?"

"Not marijuana yet, not so far as I know. But what do I know? To know what's happening with your kids these days you have to take a course in criminal investigation. And interrogation too. You're the expert on motivation. Why is all this? What the hell do they want?"

"Look, what did we want when we were kids? To do better than our fathers. What did we have? Nothing we didn't get ourselves. That took a lot of energy, a lot of time. There wasn't anything left for this kind of nonsense. We made things too easy for our kids, you know that as well as I do."

"So what's the answer? You can't manufacture the old conditions."

"The answer? Watch them and pray, pray they don't do too much damage to themselves until they're on their own. And then you pray they *will* be on their own. How many men do you know who are still kicking in something every month to a divorced daughter? Or a married daughter. It makes no difference."

"Quite a few."

"Exactly. My father used to be afraid there'd be no one to take care of him in his old age. Maybe that's why he dropped dead when he was fifty. Now it's getting to be the other way around. Can you make enough money until the end so you can support your children and *their* families in the style to which you've accustomed them? We could be trapped, Sam. Trapped for good."

DON MARTURANO:

We're the first generation of the affluent society and don't really have to worry about where the next meal's coming from, so that we can be more idealistic than those people were in the past.

INTERVIEWER:
Do you think today's kids take economic security too much for granted?

MR. FLOWERS:

Yes, yes, I think they rely entirely upon—you're just supposed to do it. A child asks you, "Daddy, I want to go to the bowling alley." Well, that's three bucks to go to the bowling alley. And that's all. He doesn't think about going to work to get it. You can't get him to pick up the coke bottles and take 'em down and get three cents for them. He thinks that that's your responsibility. That's the way— he has not learned to work. We haven't trained him to work. We haven't trained him to save. He just feels that somebody ought to do it.

MR. McGRAW:

Success, in my day, I think, was perhaps getting away from poverty and having enough bread and beans and potatoes on the table and meat, so that your family could eat. Today the children have never gone through this. We were told when I was a senior at the University of Nebraska that we could expect to start out at $75 or $100 a month.

ADVERTISING AGE
March 10, 1969

'68 Teen Spending Hit $20 Billion, Rand Bureau Says

NEW YORK, March 4— Teen spending power was freely exercised last year as America's 28,000,000 teens plunked down $20 billion at sales counters, proving (if there was ever any doubt about it) that while dad may know how to make it, the kids know how to spend it.

Figures compiled by the Rand Youth Bureau show that girls 16 through 19 outspent their male counterparts $16.85 per week (on an income of $19.50) to $15.65 (on an income of $18.35). Leading spending categories for the fairer sex were $4.20 on clothing, $2.65 on cosmetics and fragrances, $2.15 on movies and entertainment and $1.95 on beauty parlor appointments and hair products. Boys spent $4.45 on movies and dating, $3.25 on gas and autos, $3.10 on clothing and $1.25 on candy, ice cream and soda.

In the 13 through 15 age bracket, girls again outspent the boys, this time $4.95 per week (on an income of $5.80) to $4.85 (on an income of $5.65).

■ Other findings showed that the teen population is increasing at the rate of 1,000,000 per year and that parttime work is one of the reasons for the spiraling spending trend ($5 billion in 1950; $12 billion in 1959, and almost double that total today). #

C   Bb   C   Bb   G

Ever say you loved 'em Ever let 'em watch you drink Ever wonder why Your

daughter looked so sad it's such a drag to have to love a plastic Mom & Dad

Verse 2: Mama! Mama! Your child was killed in the park today
          Shot by the cops as she quietly lay

          By the side of the creeps she knew....
          They killed her too.

The young shall be silent before their elders and
give them place, and rise up before them. —Plato

39

The Grown-up Problem

By ART BUCHWALD

There has been so much discussion about teen-age problems that the grown-up problem is practically being ignored. And yet if you pick up a newspaper, you realize grown-ups are responsible for some of the most serious problems this country has ever faced.

For example, 60 percent of all crime in the United States is committed by grown-ups.

The birth rate among grown-up women is four times that of teen-agers.

The divorce rate is double.

The purchasing power of grown-ups almost exceeds that of teen-agers.

Grown-ups are responsible for more daytime accidents than any other age group.

The source of these statistics is sociology Prof. Heinrich Applebaum, B.A., M.S., LL.D., Y.E.H., Y.E.H., Y.E.H., who told me in an exclusive interview that his studies showed grown-ups were drifting farther away from society all the time.

"The average grown-up," Prof. Applebaum said, "feels his children don't understand him. The more time he spends with them, the less they communicate with him. So the adult feels isolated, insecure, and misunderstood. In defense he seeks out other grown-ups who feel the same way he does. Pretty soon they form gangs, go to the theater together, hold cocktail parties and dances, and before you know it you have a complete breakdown of the family."

"Why do you think grown-ups are constantly rebelling against their children, Professor?"

"I guess it's an age-old old-age problem. You have parents wanting to break away and yet not having the nerve to cut the ties completely. Grown-ups are afraid to stand up to their children, so they rebel against society instead."

"Do you think teen-agers could in some way be responsible for the behavior of their parents?"

"I definitely do," the Professor said. "Grown-ups try to emulate teen-agers. They want to do exactly what teen-agers do, which is to drink, smoke, and drive fast cars. If teen-agers didn't do these things, their parents wouldn't. For every bad adult in America, I'm sure you'll find a bad teen-ager somewhere in the background."

"Where do you think the trouble starts?"

"In the home. Teen-agers are too rough on their par-

ents. They're always criticizing them for listening to Frank Sinatra records and reading **Holiday** magazine. Teen-agers don't have any patience with their mothers and fathers. They can't understand why their parents like Doris Day and Rock Hudson movies or what they see in Cary Grant. If teen-agers spent more time with grown-ups and tried to understand them, I don't think you'd have half the trouble that you have in the United States today."

"Do you mean teen-agers should spend more time at home with their parents?"

"Of course. Grown-ups need security. They want to know where their children are. They want the feeling they belong. Only teen-agers can give grown-ups this feeling."

"Professor, have you found any homes where grown-ups are leading healthy, normal, secure lives, thanks to the attention they've received from their loving teen-age children?"

"We haven't yet. But we've been looking only a year. These surveys take time."

Communication Exercise

1. This inventory is an exercise designed to help you and your parents better understand how you communicate with each other. Most teen-agers find it very interesting.
2. There are no right or wrong answers. The most helpful answer to each question is your indication of the way you feel at the moment.
3. The YES column is to be used when the question can be answered as happening <u>most of the time</u> or <u>usually</u>. The NO column is to be used when the question can be answered as <u>seldom</u> or <u>never</u>. Draw a circle around the word YES or NO, whichever reflects your answer.
4. Read each question carefully. If you cannot give the exact answer to a question, answer as best you can but be sure to <u>answer each one</u>.

1. Do your parents wait until you are through talking before "having their say"? — (YES)   NO

2. Does your family do things as a group? — (YES)   NO

3. Does your family talk things over with each other? — (YES)   NO

4. Do your parents seem to respect your opinion? — (YES)   NO

5. Do your parents tend to lecture and preach too much to you? — YES   (NO)

6. Do you discuss personal problems with either of your parents? — YES   (NO)

7. Do your parents tend to talk to you as if you were much younger than you actually are? — (YES)   NO

8. Do they show an interest in your interests and activities? — (YES)   NO

9. Do you discuss matters of sex with either of your parents? — YES   (NO)

10. Do your parents trust you? — YES   (NO)

11. Do you find it hard to say what you feel at home? — YES   (NO)

12. Do your parents have confidence in your abilities? — (YES)   NO

42

13. Do you hesitate to disagree with either of them?	YES	(NO)
14. Do you fail to ask your parents for things because you feel they'll deny your requests?	(YES)	NO
15. Do they really try to see your side of things?	(YES)	NO
16. Do your parents consider your opinion in making decisions which concern you?	(YES)	NO
17. Do they try to make you feel better when you're down in the dumps?	YES	(NO)
18. Do your parents explain their reason for not letting you do something?	(YES)	NO
19. Do you ask them their reasons for the decisions they make concerning you?	(YES)	NO
20. Do you help your parents to understand you by telling them how you think and feel?	(YES)	NO

NOW COMPLETE THESE STATEMENTS:

What worries me most about my future is_____
_____.

The main weakness of American parents is_____
_____.

The most difficult subject to discuss with my parents is_____
_____.

What I want most out of life is_____
_____.

Now that you have finished the exercise, the next step is to discuss it with your parents as soon as the three of you are able to sit down together without any interruptions. Your parents should ask you why you chose the answers you did. The more you talk the more they learn. Encourage them to continue similar discussions.

"I think it's really hard for a lot of
parents to understand that there is just a
different viewpoint altogether, a different life
style coming into being."

3.
Life Styles

MISS McWATTERS: I think it's really hard for a lot of parents to understand that there is just a different viewpoint altogether, a different life style coming into being.

CBS

DR. MARTURANO: To me, it's sort of, it's nauseating. It's disgusting. I think grooming and cleanliness, taking care of oneself, I mean, this is important, I mean, in everyday life. I don't like these liberties these youngsters take in their dress.

PAT STIMER: I'm absolutely amazed at how upset people are about long hair. And it's just like, the last hundred years is the first time in human history that people have cut their hair short.

Dear Abby

Judge His Habits, Not His Hair

DEAR ABBY: I am the mother of two teen-aged boys who wear their hair too long to suit me. I recently saw an ad in a Connecticut newspaper which read as follows: "WANTED—BOY. Must be 17 years of age. Must have normal haircut."

Abby, if all employers would hire only boys with normal haircuts, I am quite sure we would have our boys looking like boys again instead of like freaks.

I also blame the girls for the long hair look on boys. My sons tell me the girls LIKE boys to wear their hair long.

SIGN ME DISGUSTED

DEAR DISGUSTED: There are more battles raging in the modern American home because of "hair" than any other one area of conflict, and I say it's foolish. Personally, I don't like long hair on boys, either, but I still say that if a boy keeps his hair clean and is a good citizen, he has earned the right to wear his hair the way he wants to.

A fine head of hair adds beauty to a good face, and terror to an ugly one.—**Lycurgus**

MOVIE MAILBAG
'Just Too Much'

To the Editor:

Recent letters in the Movie Mailbag concerning "Alice's Restaurant" and "Easy Rider" bring up a subject that deserves more than the simplistic treatment it has been given. They write about young people being "victimized" for the way they look, or the way they dress, and decry the "prejudice" that causes ordinary people to be angered by the presence of the long-haired young.

The question involved, however, is not individual dress but symbolic speech. If one young person blew into town with, say, a shaved head, I doubt that he would evoke more than curiosity and perhaps good-natured (or not so good-natured) ribbing. It would be assumed that he was, in the current parlance, doing his own thing. But the long-haired unkempt young things who so arouse the public are a different phenomenon entirely. They are not individualists. They are wearing a uniform (albeit a sloppy one). Their reason for wearing it appears, to the man in the street, to be a gesture of contempt for their parents, their elders, their homes, their country. Their dirtiness and contrived ugliness seem to bespeak a lack of respect for themselves, as well as for others.

To people whose lives have been struggles to maintain the thin veneer of civilization and civility that covers man's irrationality, the sight of the children of affluence, the hope of the future, sinking to the depths of what appears to be animal degradation is Just Too Much! Aren't we demanding too much of human beings to expect them to respond with benevolent tolerance to what appears to be a gesture of utter contempt for all that is meaningful to them?

It sometimes seems that the ordinary people have more feeling for art than today's artists. Is not art the bringing of order out of chaos, beauty out of ugliness? I don't think we should blame the young people for their symbolic speech: I doubt that most of them realize the implications of their anarchic ways. But the artists who should be leading them to a higher civilization seem to be pied pipers of barbarism.

What a man looks like should not enter into our evaluation of him. It is a trivial matter, at best. But if he chooses to use his appearance as a form of expression, he cannot complain if someone disagrees with his presence.

The symbolic speech of dress is a "cop out." Let these young people articulate their ideas, as they certainly have a right to do. They will then be open to refutation and counterargument. A dialogue may ensue and people on both sides might learn something. As long as the discourse is carried on by means of gestures, we cannot expect it to rise above the level of pre-verbal man, i.e., infants.

Joyce P. Davis, Teaneck, N. J.

How do you tell the girls from the boys?

Once upon a time, all you had to do was look.
But that was once upon a time.
Today, more than ever, a feminine fragrance is

almost essential. Toward
this end, we suggest My Sin.
It does what
dropping a handkerchief
used to do.

MY SIN by Lanvin
A quiet statement of femininity

Face to Face

with Miss Black America

The same night that the new Miss (white) America tearfully accepted her crown, nineteen-year-old Saundra Williams, of Philadelphia, Pennsylvania, also held court in Atlantic City. She smiled for photographers and talked with newsmen about her new title—Miss Black America.

"What a night! It was like an impossible dream coming true," she recalls. "For years I'd been brainwashed into thinking that beauty consisted of straight hair, a thin, straight nose and thin lips. The contest proved what I'd recently learned—black *is* beautiful."

Saundra grew up in a comfortable middle-class family; her mother is a caterer, her father an electrical engineer. "I went to an integrated high school and never considered the black-white thing. I had close friends of both races and we did everything together—until we went home. But I never really questioned why my neighborhood was black and theirs was white. I guess I just accepted the idea that this was how things were."

Saundra received a sudden awakening when she went away to college. "I was accustomed to big city life with its freedom, so Maryland State College in Princess Anne was an entirely new experience. There was discrimination. We couldn't eat in a local restaurant because they wouldn't serve blacks. There was no such thing as 'your friend the policeman.' And I saw members of the Ku Klux Klan burn a cross. I just couldn't understand why they did it; they turned the symbol of Christianity, of love, into something hateful."

The friendly, relaxed, integrated atmosphere of Saundra's high school days in Philadelphia seemed very far away. "I had never really identified with my people because I was somewhat isolated. But suddenly I wanted to learn about my race, and I read everything I could get my hands on. *The Autobiography of Malcolm X* had a tremendous influence on me; it made me realize that the black people were my people, that I wasn't an island. It really changed me."

Saundra had always had her hair straightened. "I never consciously imitated white people. It seemed the natural thing to do, like tweezing my eyebrows. But early last summer, I washed my hair, let it go and loved it. When I looked in the mirror, I found the real me! In a sense, of course, it's a form of protest. The white man says, 'If you want to be accepted, think as I think and dress as I dress. You'll never be as good as me, but try.' Natural hair styles and African clothing are the black people's way of showing their individuality. They can look as good as whites, but on their own terms. A black man can compete on all levels with a white man. He's himself now, not some second-rate imitation."

51

MR. McGRAW: Well, of course, I dislike long hair and I dislike seeing boys go out on dates without being dressed up or without a girl wearing a dress but we used to put on the very best thing we had each day when we went to school.

Everybody's youth is a dream,

...a form of chemical madness.
—**F. Scott Fitzgerald**

some touch of madness.
—**Seneca**

THE NEW YORK TIMES

TEACH ROCK?

TO THE EDITOR:

Let me give you some reasons why I, as a Music Departmental Chairman in the New York City High Schools, would not teach nor permit the teaching of "rock" in my classes.

I have always believed it to be the prime and major function of the school to open the minds of children to things above and beyond the meretricious and the temporal. In my 50-odd years, association with music, 20 of which were spent in the profession, I have witnessed the passing of many musical fancies—ragtime, swing, blues, Dixieland, modern jazz and so on. They came and went as they always will come and go. Why, then, should I waste the taxpayers' money, the children's time and my energies teaching something which they could easily learn without my intervention—something about which, in all probability, they already know as much as there is to know?

The presumption that composers could learn something from jazz and rock is pure nonsense. Technically, these idioms are about 50 years behind the times. You will pardon me for adding that I consider myself pragmatically, academically and chronologically qualified to make that statement.

HARRY A. FELDMAN
Music Chairman, N.Y.C.H.S.
(Retired)

TO THE EDITOR:

In a recent letter, Harry A. Feldman, a retired New York City High School Music Chairman, stated that he "would not teach or permit the teaching" of rock or jazz in his classes because he "believed it the prime and major function of the school to open the minds of children to things above and beyond the meretricious and temporal."

It would be nice to think that Mr. Feldman is atypical of the New York City school system. Unfortunately, my own experience suggests that his attitude is all too typical of much of the professional staff in the New York schools. Every week of the school year brings dozens of complaints to the offices of the New York Civil Liberties Union from students in difficulty because they edit "seditious" newspapers or wear their hair long, or from teachers facing transfer for suggesting books by Malcolm X or Eldridge Cleaver to their classes.

Is it any wonder that our schools are in turmoil? And isn't it possibly a good thing?

ARYEH NEIER
Executive Director,
New York Civil
Liberties Union

New York City

language of jazz musicians (1958)

cut, *v. i. & t.* (1) (intr.) To leave. Usually to "cut out" (cut = leave out, leave). "Man, nothin's happening, let's cut out!" (2) (tr.) To play an instrument better than another musician, or to produce better jazz than another. Also said of whole orchestras. The winner in a musical contest is said to have "cut" the other.

cute, *adv.* (Playing) in an ingenious, intriguing manner. Occ., in an amusing manner.

dig, *v.* To understand and agree with: not limited to music alone. (Perhaps fr. a sense of "getting to the bottom" of things.)

end, the, *n.* The best, the most pleasing. Like *most* (q.v.), but better. *Absolute end, n.*, intensified form.

eyes, *n.* An expression denoting approval. "I've got eyes for that" means "I like it." Extreme approval is expressed by the qualifying words "big" or "bulging." Invented by Lester Young.

fake, *v.* To improvise (see p. 41). Sometimes also means to pretend to know a tune, but usually has meaning above.

flip, *v.* To approve wildly. Orig. to "flip one's wig" (akin to "blow one's top," but never denotes anger for jazzmen). Usually indicates response to another's solo.

funky, *n.* An old word, orig. meaning earthy or odorous. Now, a piece or player imbued with the basic spirit of the blues, although in a modern idiom.

gas, *v. & n.* To please, or, as noun, spoken of a situation which pleases—"It's a gas!" *gasser, n.* Something which pleases extremely. Origin unknown, at least to me.

go, *expl.* Really a fan's word, to express excitement at a particularly "swingin'" solo. Often used derisively, sometimes approvingly, by musicians. (The fan's full phrase is "Go, man, go!")

gone, *adj.* In the ultimate state of happiness, usually inspired by music. *Real gone, adj.*, intensified form. (Perhaps from dope addiction, but it is equally possible that the borrowing went the other way.) Occ., older. the gonest, *n. The most*, etc.

goof, *n. & v.* A mistake in playing, and to make that mistake. Extended to all errors.

greatest, *n.* See *most, end.*

Little Oxford Dictionary

By GLORIA EMERSON

LONDON, Oct. 16 — The editors of the Little Oxford Dictionary would not cringe to hear that they are indeed with it, for clearly they mean to be.

The fourth edition of the 39-year-old dictionary, published here last week, shows on page 658 that "with it" has won through.

A new, somber respectability also settles on other words that started with the young and now seem middle-aged. There are "swinging" (up-to-the-minute), "fix," "dropout" and "hippy," defined as a "person (appearing to be) given to the use of hallucinogenic drugs; a hipster."

There are three pages of addenda—"the editor's desperate last thoughts," as The Guardian described them—which include not only "hippy" but also "fuzz" (police), "hot line" (permanently open telephone connection) and "dicey" (risky, dangerous).

There are also "do-it-yourself," "caftan" (a woman's loosely hanging dress) "backlash," "admass" (part of community easily influenced by mass publicity), "banger" (sausage; noisy old car) and "permissive," as in "permissive society."

Compared with the newcomers, the slang word "copper," for policeman, has a nice old-fashioned feeling to it. So does "turkeycock" (strutting pompous person) and "chump" (coloquial for blockhead).

"There is no stopping time's swing-winged chariot when it comes to popular jargon," The Times of London observed.

The Little Oxford is the smallest of the Oxford family of five. It has 684 pages and is five by three and three-quarters inches in size. The policy of its editions has always been to admit new words "whose place and dignity in the language were less assured" than those words entered into its fatter, stricter relatives.

Senior and most authoritative is the Oxford English Dictionary. It fills 13 volumes, costs $192 and has not been revised since its completion in 1928.

The other Oxford dictionaries are the Pocket, the Concise, and the Shorter Oxford English Dictionary.

While "miniskirt" and "module," "splashdown" and "retrorocket," "finalize" and "the pill" also make their first appearance, omissions leap to mind.

Cool, smashing, groovy, a gas, topless, body stocking, a trip and happening are some of them.

Also missing are bag, scene, split level and thing (as in doing your).

"Misbegotten monsters" is what a columnist for The Times of London chooses to call some of the "vogue words" that he fears may achieve permanence. They are not unpredictably, "parking-meter," "wage freeze," "cha-risma," "starch-reduced," "broiler-house" and "escalate."

Others might object to "de-briefing" (examination or in-terrogation after completion of mission) or resent the intru-sion of the language from the computer world. Such as "hardware" and "printouts."

The omission of four-letter words included in the Penguin English Dictionary first pub-lished here in 1965, and in the Random House Dictionary of the English Language, publish-ed in New York in 1968, have not caused comment.

The Little Oxford, which costs the equivalent of about $1.10 here, has an annual sale of about 250,000.

Slang is the language that takes off its coat, spits on its hands, and goes to work.

—Carl Sandburg

"Crazy!"   "Crazy!"

*I'm all for love —
I want it to last.*

4.
A New
Morality?

Teen-Age Decency Rally Draws 30,000 In Miami

MIAMI, March 23.—Some 30,000 hand-clapping persons, some waving signs saying "Down With Obscenity," rallied in the Orange Bowl today to support a teenage crusade for decency in entertainment.

Teen-agers organized the rally after Jim Morrison, 24 years old, the lead singer of The Doors, a rock group, was charged with indecent exposure during a concert in Miami on March 1. Six warrants have been issued for Mr. Morrison's arrest.

Mike Levesque, 17, the originator of the rally, a senior at Miami Springs High School, said the idea had grown out of a Roman Catholic youth group discussion two days after the concert by The Doors.

"This is not a protest rally," said Julie James, 18, a member of the teen-age Rally for Decency. "We're not against something. We're for something."

Talks on God and Sex

Teen-age speakers gave three-minute talks on God, parents, patriotism, sexuality and brotherhood. There were appearances by professional entertainers, who donated their time.

"Five virtues," selected as the keynote of the rally, were "belief in God and that He loves us; love of our planet and country; love of our family; reverence of one's sexuality, and equality of all men."

"Sex is definitely being exploited and it is because society has been losing its reverence for one's sexuality," Miss James said.

The shirt-sleeved crowd basking in a warm sun cheered for Jackie Gleason, Anita Bryant and The Lettermen, popular music singers, who appeared in order to applaud the teenage rally.

"I believe this kind of movement will snowball across the United States and perhaps around the world," Mr. Gleason said.

"I think it's great, there should be more things like that," said Tony Butala of The Lettermen.

Young Levesque said he was thrilled by the rapid growth of the decency movement and the support it had gained from adults.

The crowd was about evenly split between teen-agers and adults.

Another member of the executive committee, Alan Rosenthal, 16, said telephone calls and letters had come in from around the country from teenage groups interested in the movement.

He said: "We're going to try to come up with some kind of international youth organization. It could really tie the world together.

"The youths start out with something like this, and 10 years from now when they get a little older, who knows what could happen."

Numerous organizations, including major religious denominations, contributed to the rally. Members of the American Legion passed out 10,000 small American flags.

Responsibility Of Youth

COMPLAINTS are many, and warranted, that we are recklessly and unfairly passing on to our successors a mammoth and burdensome public debt.

But segments of the generation consisting of today's young men and women in the late-'teens and early-twenties might well be asked what sort of heritage they may be preparing for their successors—and, indeed, for themselves in their own maturity.

A group of New York doctors have published further documentation of the familiar fact of increasing sexual promiscuity. Their reports appear in the New York State Journal of Medicine.

The erstwhile respectably high percentage of virgins among brides has markedly declined, with a corresponding increase in the number of men who have had sexual experience before marriage. And now, one out of every 18 babies is born out of wedlock.

The doctors have re-enforced the many evidences of the new looseness and have concluded, as have others, that youth is undergoing a revolution in its attitudes towards sex, life and proper behavior.

When we deplore this, as we have before, it is not out of prudish unawareness of the times or blindness to the force of passion. It is in the knowledge of the history of the human family, a knowledge which includes the futility and the tragedy of such uninhibited foolhardiness, with its tendency to create general insecurity.

It is popular to blame parents for the unbridled youth of the era, and they are not without guilt to be sure. But at the age of indulgence the young people who are the subject of the doctors' report should be taking on an obligation of their own in this matter — in their own behalf and in behalf of those they will present to this world.

As things are going now, the consequences will be worse than the monetary debt they will inherit. Enlightened youth is not without its own responsibility for today and tomorrow.

number of births out of wedlock

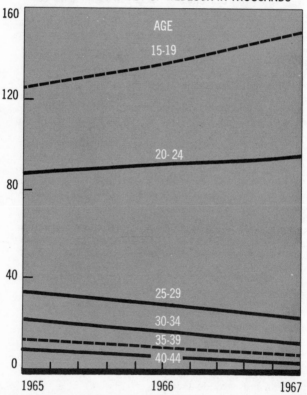

NUMBER OF BIRTHS OUT OF WEDLOCK IN THOUSANDS

AGE
15-19
20-24
25-29
30-34
35-39
40-44

160
120
80
40
0

1965   1966   1967

Source: Department of Health, Education, and Welfare, Office of Child Development

Out of the everywhere into the here.
—George Macdonald

Illegitimacy rate

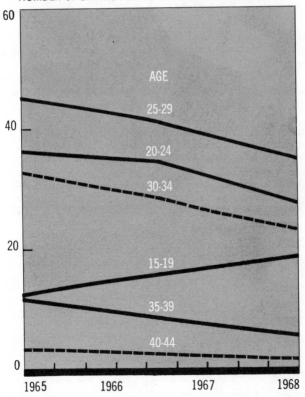

NUMBER OF BIRTHS PER 1.000 UNMARRIED WOMEN

AGE
25-29
20-24
30-34
15-19
35-39
40-44

CBS

MRS. O'DONNELL: Well, I happen to be —I guess people might even call me Victorian. I don't know. But very conservative in this one area. I believe a happier marriage results from young people who have waited.

MISS McWATTERS: I think really it's a necessary part of growing up—I mean, it's one of life's most beautiful experiences. And I do not see the reason that people say, well, I know their rationalizations, like, you should wait until you are really in love and this is the person you're going to spend the rest of your life with. See, because people are so afraid of being hurt, that they think if they have a beautiful relationship for one year and then you decide that you're going to go your own way, that that's just terrible, you know. Like, they want the security, not the love, they want the security of one person and therefore, they say, wait, don't give yourself to anybody, give yourself to the person who's going to stick with you and give you the security that you need. And I just—I don't know—I can't go along with that.

JOY BEAMON: This in my thinking is a privilege after you're married, not before. This might have been the way I was brought up, but this is one thing my folks taught all of us kids pretty well — sat down and talked with us and you might say drilled it into our heads. But to have — to come home to my parents right now and say, "Mom, I'm pregnant," I'd never be able to do it. I couldn't face my folks because I know it's wrong.

Ann Landers' Advice

DEAR ANN LANDERS: I'm so ashamed I can hardly hold up my head. Last night my boyfriend and I went too far. Not all the way, but nearly. We were in the rec room downstairs and the lights were off. Mom thought we were still out to a movie and she came downstairs with a flashlight because she thought she heard some noise. Of course, she caught us. She looked so hurt it nearly killed me. Thank heaven she was very calm and didn't yell or anything. She asked Harvey to leave while she talked to me. Harvey insisted on staying. He said it was more his fault than mine and that he wanted to face the lecture with me. Honestly, Ann, he was wonderful. Harvey apologized and asked Mom to give us another chance. He promised we would never do anything like that again if she would let us keep seeing each other. Her decision was that we could date, but not steady. She said I'd have to go with other boys and that Harvey should date other girls.

Ann, I don't want to go with anyone else. I love Harvey and he loves me. We are both 16 and have been going steady for 14 months. Please help us convince Mom we can be trusted and that she should give us another chance.

BALTIMORE BLUES

...this world is a hard place for girls.
—**Martin Luther**

Friday the 4th

I've been reading a book on the psychology of the unwed mother. I saw it downstairs and couldn't help picking it up. I guess the house of a sociology professor isn't the best place to stay, if you are expecting a baby out of wedlock and would rather not think about it for a while.

The book says such a pregnancy is rarely accidental. It says the girl nearly always wants it—as a crutch, an excuse to fail, a way to rebel or demonstrate against her parents or other authority she felt she never could free herself from. Also the book says unmarried mothers often keep their babies because they are emotionally immature and unable to face reality. Phew, that sounds like a mouthful, as if the author is really looking for symptoms where there aren't any. That couldn't possibly be all true. Of course, maybe in some instances, but not in mine.

I admit I was beginning to make bad grades. But I couldn't have been afraid of failure; my teachers always said I should apply myself, that I am bright enough. I made straight A's through my sophomore year but then school started making less and less sense to me. In a crazy way I'm almost glad I don't have to go to school next year. I need time to think things over, decide what I want to do with myself. I thought I might want to go on and get a master's degree in psychology and be a social worker. Do something about this mixed-up world we live in. The way things are—one little war after another, riots, and millions starving in India and all that—I don't know what there is to believe in.

I guess Daddy thinks I'm a lost cause. He thinks I don't know who I am and where I'm going. Hell, he's the one who wanted me to come here instead of going to college at home. For once we agreed. I don't think I could stand going to school where he is teaching. What used to bug me was the way his students used to tell me how lucky I was to have a father like him. They said he gave such good advice and always had time to listen. Little did they know that whenever we got into a discussion about anything at home it always turned into an argument. Daddy thought I ought to be number one in my class, and he thought I brought absolute disgrace on the family because my friends grew beards and wore sandals and played guitars.

I think my friends are real people. They are natural because they don't want to pretend. Why should we wear make-up to look like something we're not? Why should we cut our hair when obviously it keeps growing? So Daddy called it childish and immature—a failure to cope with realities. Because we don't make believe and pretend all is well with a phony world.

By that standard, maybe I am a failure the way the book says. But I didn't want to get pregnant. If I did, I'd be happy as a lark now, wouldn't I, instead of in a mess?

. I know me, Put me in with a bunch of straights, I turn hippie, with a bunch of hippies I am STRAIGHT as a rule. I can't conform — not right down the line. I've tried great - I don't believe in it — I hate to have control — I want to live my life, not

72

worse — I always get sick. Throwing up in somebody's toilet is not my idea of a night of fun. I wouldn't even touch hard drugs — I've got enough problems. I'm all for love — I want it to last. I guess I want the best of both worlds — stimulation with responsibility.

73

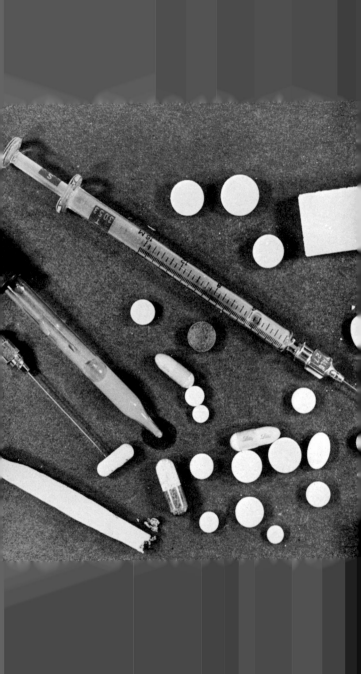

"If only I had known six weeks ago what I am beginning to find out now, I am sure my darling son would be alive today."

5.
Drugs

FEDERAL NARCOTIC DRUG
AND MARIHUANA LAWS
MARIHUANA
I. IMPORTATION

A. Under 21 U.S.C. 176a, it is unlawful to import or bring into the United States any marihuana contrary to law—knowingly and with intent to defraud the United States. Alternatively, it is unlawful to smuggle or clandestinely introduce into the United States any marihuana which should have been invoiced—knowingly and with intent to defraud the United States.

1. Section 176a also prohibits receiving, concealing, buying, selling, or in any manner facilitating the transportation, concealment or sale of such marihuana after it has been imported or brought in—knowing that it was imported or brought into the United States contrary to law.

2. Conspiring to accomplish any of the proscribed acts is also an offense.

3. The Section sets up a permissive inference of guilt based solely on unexplained possession of marihuana.

4. The penalty for a first offense under Section 176a is not less than five nor more than twenty years' imprisonment. In addition, the offender may be fined not more than $20,000. For a second or subsequent offense, the offender will be imprisoned for not less than ten nor more than forty years and, in addition, may be fined not more than $20,000.

B. 21 U.S.C. 184a makes it an offense for anyone to bring on board, or have in his possession or control on board any vessel of the United States which is engaged in a foreign voyage, any mari-

Parents Obey Law, So Girl Is Arrested For Using a Drug

BRYN ATHYN, Pa., Jan. 21 (AP)— "We have to live within the law," said the millionaire parents of a teenager in explaining why they had their daughter arrested for possessing and using marijuana.

"It was the only thing to do," said Mrs. Jean Pitcairn. Her husband, Lachlan, is treasurer of the Pitcairn Company, which is a principal shareholder of the Pittsburgh Plate Glass Company.

Fawn Pitcairn, 18 years old, the third oldest of their seven children, was arrested just before New Year's Eve after a boyfriend delivered a belated Christmas gift containing marijuana. She pleaded guilty in Montgomery County Court and was placed on 18 months' probation and ordered to earn her $300 fine.

"I think we parents of this generation have to face this drug problem," Mrs. Pitcairn said in an interview. "I think the important thing we have to try to do is make young people realize the seriousness of the drug situation. The enforcement of the law is a powerful way to get through to them the seriousness of it."

Mrs. Pitcairn, who is 46, as is her husband, said she believed "a lot of people are in accord with us," and added, "If all parents get together, we can handle this."

Jack Hopson, a state narcotics agent who investigated the case, said: "It is gratifying to see parents who are aware of the problems of drugs of all types being used by teen-agers."

SOME CHARACTERISTICS OF 114 LSD users

Average age	23 (range 15-43)
Male	68.4%
White	88.4%
LSD 1-3 times only	72.8%
Overwhelming panic	13.1%
Violence	12.3%
Homicidal or suicidal	8.6%
Underlying overt mental disease	34.2%
Requiring extended hospitalization	15.8%

OCCUPATIONAL HISTORY
68 cases

Student	15
High School	6
College or graduate	9
Unemployed	12
Writer, artist, musician, photographer	11
Cook, waiter, caterer	7
Welder, carpenter, printer	5
Model, dancer	5
Physician, engineer, pharmacist	4
Sociologist, teacher	4
Typist, beautician	2
Housewife	2
Rancher	1

Food and Drug Administration

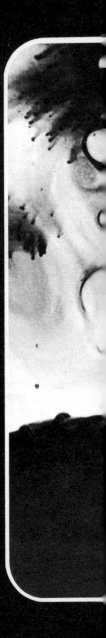

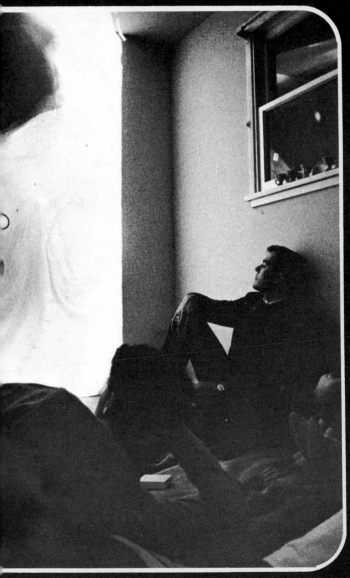

I know how men in exile feed on dreams . . .
　　　　　　　　　　　　　　　—Aeschylus

"Pot party tonight at Lisl Camp's," Dex said, happily. "Her folks are out of town and we'll have the whole place to ourselves." He laughed. "Lisl is staying with Betty Dermott while her parents are away, but she's got the key to her own house, of course. We're going to meet over there about eight o'clock. If you'd like to go, I'll pick you up."

"Won't Betty's parents wonder where she and Lisl are?" I'd wondered the thought aloud.

Dexter laughed again. "Nothing to worry about. *They* think the girls are staying all night with Doris Denman, and Doris's parents don't care what time *anybody* gets home." Suddenly, he frowned. "What's it to you, anyway? If you don't like the arrangement you don't need to go."

"But I want to go!" I was really anguished.

"Of course, you do." Dex was smiling again. "That's the power of pot. You just start thinking about it, and all your little scruples go down the drain."

I knew that Dexter was speaking in fun, but it upset me a little, too. Thinking about the light, happy, kind of crazy feeling I got when I was smoking pot was what had made me forget that it wasn't right for Lisl Camp to be having a bunch of kids in her house when her parents were out of town.

I heard Dexter's car in the drive, and for the second time that day I pushed the thought from my mind.

My mother had opened the door before I could

get downstairs. I noticed that she had changed from the slacks and sweater she'd had on at dinner to the new floor-length wool hostess gown she'd bought to replace the gold corduroy. I'd not seen that one since the night I'd come home from Glenna's house and found her drunk. Like the gold one, this one was made with some kind of fullness in the back. I think she knew it made her look like a princess. She was holding out both hands to Dexter who, I was pleased to see, looked very nice. At least he had not gotten himself up in the rather odd fashion in which he sometimes comes to school.

"You're Dexter Smith," said my mother, then added with a little smile, "Carla's told me all about you."

"She's told me all about you, too, Mrs. Devon." Dexter's manner was both engaging and boyish. I could see my mother was charmed. Certainly, she never suspected just how much Dexter knew.

"Won't you sit down, Dexter? Carla will be down presently."

I said, "I'm down," and my mother said, "Oh, there you are!" as if she'd not noticed me on the stairs a moment before. She sighed prettily. "Well, I suppose you two will want to be running along to your party."

"I'm afraid we have to," Dexter said. Somehow he managed to sound genuinely regretful. "It's nice here, though. Perhaps some other time."

THE HARTFORD TIMES

Anthony Shapiro, 18, Victim of Drug Dose

WEST HARTFORD — Anthony Colin Shapiro, 18, of Brownleigh Road, died Sunday from an overdose of unknown drugs.

The youth was found dead in his bedroom in the afternoon, and the medical examiner's preliminary report stated he died in his sleep "from an accidental drug overdose, drug unknown."

A youth who may have given Shapiro the drug was arrested late Sunday night by local detectives. His name was withheld because he is a juvenile. The youth, who lives in West Hartford, will be released into the custody of his parents and the case has been referred to juvenile authorities.

The medical examiner said blood tests might determine the drug causing death, but the state laboratory will not have the results for about six weeks.

Born in Birmingham, England, Shapiro lived in West Hartford for 12 years. He was graduated from Conard High School in 1969 and was a member of Congregation Teferes Israel.

He leaves his parents, Lional and Evelyn Kloss Shapiro, a brother, Michael, and a sister, Miss Kim Beverley Shapiro, all of West Hartford and his maternal grandparents, Louis and Ann Motzney Kloss of London.

The funeral will be at 12:30 p.m. Tuesday in the chapel of Weinstein Mortuary, 640 Farmington Ave., with Rabbi Haskel Lindenthal officiating. There will be no calling hours.

Memorial week will be observed at the home of his parents.

My son, if sinners entice thee, consent thou not.

Proverbs 1, 10

Juvenile, 15, Held In Fatal Drug Sale

WEST HARTFORD—Police have charged a 15-year-old local boy with selling a drug to another town youth who later died of an apparent overdose.

According to Police Chief William P. Rush, the boy has been turned over to the state juvenile authorities.

Anthony C. Shapiro, 18, of Brownleigh Rd., died of an apparent drug overdose. A second local youth, Hyman Fritz, 19, of 5 Craigmore Rd., died three weeks later, also of an apparent drug overdose. However, Chief Rush said the arrest is not connected with the second boy's death.

Police said the arrested boy is the son of a Hartford druggist and has admitted taking the drugs, which allegedly killed Shapiro, from a supply his father had at his grandmother's home. His father was also connected with a wholesale drug firm.

Rush said the investigation is continuing into the death of Fritz.

. . . and a little child shall lead them.
—Isaiah 11, 6

36 Brownleigh Road
West Hartford, Conn. 06117

To Students Everywhere:

Twelve years ago I came to this country from England, and thought it was the most wonderful country in the world to live in. A little over four weeks ago, my beloved son Anthony, 18 years of age, died of an accidental overdose of drugs, and for a couple of weeks after the tragedy I was sorry I had ever left my homeland.

Believe me when I tell you, the worst thing that could ever happen to a parent is to lose a child. You feel as if a part of you has died forever, and no doubt, my husband and I will never get rid of that feeling.

For the past two weeks, since my mind has become more cleared, I have decided I wasn't just going to sit around and feel sorry for myself, but would do something to help both teenagers and parents understand one another better.

Since the death of my son, I have received many letters from both teenagers and parents, which opened my eyes to so many things I had no idea existed so close to home. They were just items to be read in the paper.

It was brought to my attention that even a boy or girl who wants to get help by not taking any more drugs, has to wait about eight months for a bed, which shook me quite a bit. So I am now giving a lot of my spare time helping in whatever way I can, and have already spoken to and seen a few prominent people who will help me, so that I can help others.

My mind, right now, is open for all suggestions, and I only hope that some of you reading this could give me any ideas you might have, not only for teenagers, but also for the parents, who I am sure need just as much help.

What a sad world we live in when we humans cannot sit down and talk things over.

If only I had known six weeks ago what I am beginning to find out now, I am sure my darling son would be alive today. I cannot bring him back, I only hope and pray that he has not died in vain.

Evelyn Shapiro

Evelyn Shapiro

(From a eulogy by Rabbi Stanley M. Kessler delivered at the funeral of Hyman Fritz. Mr. Fritz, a close friend of Anthony Shapiro and a pallbearer at Mr. Shapiro's funeral, died of an accidental overdose of drugs three weeks after the death of his friend.)

"Oh, Hy, I pray that your death will not be pointless, that we will turn from your grave, young and elder together, determined to build our lives and a community and a world where we will love one another the more and be honest and concerned beyond ourselves and never, never blunt our total awareness of the tasks that command a full consciousness....

"It is no secret that Hyman Fritz died of drugs. Our first impulse is to wring our hands and strike out against young people in panic and rage.... But who in our society are the main consumers of tranquilizers, pep pills, sleeping pills, brain-damaging drugs like alcohol, cancer-producing agents like cigarettes?...

"Today's youth have learned well the words love, not hate, brotherhood, non-discrimination, equal opportunity, freedom from fear and want, equality in diversity, the basic worth of the individual. . . . But the world is not like this and neither is West Hartford. . . . We are too dimmed in our vision to see our complicity with murder in Vietnam and white racists in West Hartford. Young people do see it and some scream 'hypocrisy' and others set about trying to live amidst contradictions.

"If you are less a bundle of contradictions than your parents, it's because you haven't lived as long. I don't mean this as a put-down; it's a begging. Isn't what your parents have given you as worthy of as much response as what you give your friends?

". . . Isn't using drugs symptomatic of the great cop-out? . . . If one of your friends dies as Hy died and you knew what he was doing and didn't try to move heaven and earth to stop him, isn't there a responsibility you bear?

"Do you know what you're doing . . . in creating an atmosphere of acceptability of drug use?

"There's a world out there that needs changing. You can't change it if you're high in the aura of a world not real."

mother's little helper

BY MICK JAGGER & KEITH RICHARDS
(Rolling Stones)

What a drag it is getting old
Kids are different today
I hear every mother say
Mother needs something today
to calm her down
And though she's not really ill
There's a little yellow pill.

She goes running for the shelter
of her mother's little helper
And it helps her on her way
Gets her through her busy day.

Things are different today
I hear every mother say
Cooking breakfast for her husband
Just a drag
So she buys an instant cake
And she buys a frozen steak.

And goes running for the shelter
of her mother's little helper
And it helps her on her way
Gets her through her busy day.

Doctor please some more of these
Outside the door she took four more

What a drag it is getting old.

They're just not the same today
I hear every mother say
They just don't appreciate
that you get tired
They're so hard to satisfy
You can tranquilize your mind
So go running for the shelter
of your mother's little helper
And they help you through the night
Help to minimize your plight.

Doctor please some more of these
Outside the door she took four more
What a drag it is getting old.

Life is much too hard today
I hear every mother say
The pursuit of happiness
just seems a bore;
And if you take more of those
You will get an overdose
No more running for the shelter
of your mother's little helper.
They just helped you on your way
to your busy dying day.

LACONIA, N.H., June 18—THE GANG'S ALL HERE
—Motorcycles and riders jam the main street of Weirs Beach near
Laconia, N.H. They're here for a week-end of cycle racing
at a nearby track. Seventy persons were injured when a riot broke
out on this spot one year ago.

"Look at the kid's record. At fifteen
he was in reform school. He stole a car.
He's been arrested for mugging.
He was picked up for knife fighting.
I think they said he stabbed somebody
in the arm. This is a very fine boy."

6.
Crime

300 Jersey Youths
Fight at Dance Hall

RANDOLPH TOWNSHIP, N. J., July 26 (UPI)—A discothèque session in a dance hall in this Morris County community erupted into a brawl last night and policemen from seven surrounding communities were called in to help restore the peace.

The police said 300 teen-agers at the height of the commotion were embroiled in a slugging, pushing, shouting brawl both inside and outside Polonia Acres, a big dance hall and restaurant that is used on weekends by teen-agers as a discothèque. Four teen-agers and an adult were arrested on disorderly persons charges.

The police said they did not know what touched off the fighting.

ARREST RATE PER 100,000 POPULATION

AGE	0	5,000	10,000
11-14			
15-17			
18-20			
21-24			
25-29			
30-34			
35-39			
40-44			
45-49			
50+			

Source: Department of Health, Education, and Welfare, Office of Child Development

Most car t
to be home b

Because so ma
Don't help a good boy go bac

A little neglect may breed great mischief.
—Benjamin Franklin

eves have
ore midnight.

m are under 16.
ur car. Take your keys.

OFFENSES CLEARED BY ARREST

Murder and non-negligent manslaughter
Manslaughter by negligence
Forcible rape
Robbery
Aggravated assault
Burglary—breaking and entering
Larceny—theft: Under $50.00
Larceny—theft: $50.00 and over
Auto theft

Source: Department of Health, Education, and Welfare, Office of Child Development

PERCENT WHO ARE UNDER 18

The Theifs

I went into the bike business. I am a bicycle theif. I cop and my cousin named Emilio Jerry and Ramon and me. This is a true story we play mission impossible we cop watches money and pick pocket people. I help the people and at the same time pick their pockets I steel anything I can get my hands on. We are all in school. Three of us and one works. Last time I cop $20.00 dollars from a store after I helped the man with his coat and pick pocket five dollars and here why I cop my parents don't allow me to er allowance ar give me freedom so when my big cousin ask us out we cop

STATE OF CONNECTICUT
DEPARTMENT OF ADULT PROBATION
CONDITIONS OF PROBATION

You are hereby advised that the Court may at any time revoke or modify any condition of the probation, impose any special condition it deems proper and may at any time within the period of your probation, if it sees fit, impose the judgment and sentence it might have imposed in the first instance.

During the probationary term herein fixed, you shall abide by the following terms and conditions:

FIRST,   You shall not during the term of this probation violate any criminal law of the United States, the State of Connecticut, any ordinance of a municipality of said state or the criminal law of any other state in the United States.

SECOND,   You shall not leave the State of Connecticut without the permission of the Court.

quotation

JUDGE VINCENT A. CARROLL, *of Philadelphia, urging a crackdown on teen-age gangs:* "We should bring back the old days of the whipping post. That's what these gang members need. They should be humiliated right on the public streets, with whippings, in front of the people they've been terrorizing."

THIRD, You agree to waive extradition from any state in the United States.

FOURTH, You shall report to the probation officer as he directs.

FIFTH, You shall keep your probation officer informed of your whereabouts at all times and immediately notify him of any change of address or employment.

SIXTH, You shall make all payment of monies as directed by the Court and/or the probation officer.

SEVENTH, You shall make every effort to keep yourself steadily employed and shall support those dependent upon you.

EIGHTH, You shall not engage in any anti-social conduct which shall furnish good cause for the Court to believe the probationary order should be revoked in the public interest.

It costs more to keep a man in prison than to keep a boy in college.

If you've ever complained about the high cost of higher education, consider the facts.

Four years in college cost less (about $8,000) than four years in prison ($10,760).

So why don't we send all our kids to college?

Perhaps because we won't spend the money to keep them interested in going to school

One out of three high school students doesn't stick around to graduate.

The dropout is ten times as likely to become a juvenile delinquent.

And the juvenile delinquent is perhaps a thousand times more likely to become a criminal.

It doesn't have to happen.

Good schools, with good teachers, and good facilities, can hold any youngster's interest, and turn the bad apples into good citizens.

Can we afford to spend the money for good schools?

Can we afford *not* to spend the money for good schools?

The answer will be, one way or another, a life sentence for a lot of young Americans.

NO. 6 *(Slowly)*: I don't know. I started to be convinced, you know, with the testimony from those people across the hall. Didn't they say something about an argument between the father and the boy around seven o'clock that night? I mean, I can be wrong.

NO. 11: I think it was eight o'clock. Not seven.

NO. 8: That's right. Eight o'clock. They heard the father hit the boy twice and then saw the boy walk angrily out of the house. What does that prove?

NO. 6: Well, it doesn't exactly prove anything. It's just part of the picture. I didn't say it proved anything.

FOREMAN: Anything else?

NO. 6: No.

No. 6 goes to the water fountain.

FOREMAN *(To No. 7)*: All right. How about you?

NO. 7: I don't know, most of it's been said already. We can talk all day about this thing, but I think we're wasting our time. Look at the kid's record. At fifteen he was in reform school. He stole a car. He's been arrested for mugging. He was picked up for knife-fighting. I think they said he stabbed somebody in the arm. This is a very fine boy.

NO. 8: Ever since he was five years old his father beat him up regularly. He used his fists.

NO. 7: So would I! A kid like that.

NO. 3: You're right. It's the kids. The way they are—you know? They don't listen. *(Bitter)* I've got a kid. When he was eight years old he ran away from a fight. I saw him. I was so ashamed, I told him right out, "I'm gonna make a man out of you or I'm gonna bust you up into little pieces trying." When he was fifteen he hit me in the face. He's big, you know. I haven't seen him in three years. Rotten kid! You work your heart out....*(Pause)* All right. Let's get on with it.

> *Looks away embarrassed.*

NO. 4: We're missing the point here. This boy—
let's say he's a product of a filthy neighborhood and a broken home. We can't help that.
We're not here to go into the reasons why
slums are breeding grounds for criminals.
They are. I know it. So do you. The children
who come out of slum backgrounds are po-
tential menaces to society.

NO. 10: You said it there. I don't want any part
of them, believe me.

> *There is a dead silence for a moment, and
> then No. 5 speaks haltingly.*

NO. 5: I've lived in a slum all my life—

NO. 10: Oh, now wait a second!

NO. 5: I used to play in a back yard that was
filled with garbage. Maybe it still smells on me.

FOREMAN: Now let's be reasonable. There's nothing personal—

> *No. 5 stands up.*

NO. 5: There is something personal!

> *Then he catches himself and, seeing every-
> one looking at him, sits down, fists
> clenched.*

NO. 3 (*Persuasively*): Come on, now. He didn't
mean you, feller. Let's not be so sensitive. . . .

> *There is a long pause.*

NO. 11: I can understand this sensitivity.

FOREMAN: Now let's stop the bickering. We're
wasting time. (*To No. 8*) It's your turn.

NO. 8: All right. I had a peculiar feeling about
this trial. Somehow I felt that the defense
counsel never really conducted a thorough
cross-examination. I mean, he was appointed
by the court to defend the boy. He hardly
seemed interested. Too many questions were
left unasked.

NO. 3 (*Annoyed*): What about the ones that were
asked? For instance, let's talk about that cute
little switch-knife. You know, the one that
fine, upright kid admitted buying.

NO. 8: All right. Let's talk about it. Let's get it in here and look at it. I'd like to see it again, Mr. Foreman.

The foreman looks at him questioningly and then gets up and goes to the door. During the following dialogue the foreman knocks, the guard comes in, the foreman whispers to him, the guard nods and leaves, locking the door.

NO. 3: We all know what it looks like. I don't see why we have to look at it again. *(To No. 4)* What do you think?

NO. 4: The gentleman has a right to see exhibits in evidence.

NO. 3 *(Shrugging)*: Okay with me.

NO. 4 *(To No. 8)*: This knife is a pretty strong piece of evidence, don't you agree?

NO. 8: I do.

NO. 4: The boy admits going out of his house at eight o'clock after being slapped by his father.

NO. 8: Or punched.

NO. 4: Or punched. He went to a neighborhood store and bought a switch-knife. The storekeeper was arrested the following day when he admitted selling it to the boy. It's a very unusual knife. The storekeeper identified it and said it was the only one of its kind he had in stock. Why did the boy get it? *(Sarcastically)* As a present for a friend of his, he says. Am I right so far?

NO. 8: Right.

NO. 3: You bet he's right. *(To all)* Now listen to this man. He knows what he's talking about.

NO. 4: Next, the boy claims that on the way home the knife must have fallen through a hole in his coat pocket, that he never saw it again. Now there's a story, gentlemen. You know what actually happened. The boy took the knife home and a few hours later stabbed his father with it and even remembered to wipe off the fingerprints.

The door opens and the guard walks in with an oddly designed knife with a tag on it. No. 4 gets up and takes it from him. The guard exits.

NO. 4: Everyone connected with the case identified this knife. Now are you trying to tell me that someone picked it up off the street and went up to the boy's house and stabbed his father with it just to be amusing?

NO. 8: No, I'm saying that it's possible that the boy lost the knife and that someone else stabbed his father with a similar knife. It's possible.

No. 4 flips open the knife and jams it into the table.

NO. 4: Take a look at that knife. It's a very strange knife. I've never seen one like it before in my life. Neither had the storekeeper who sold it to him.

No. 8 reaches casually into his pocket and withdraws an object. No one notices this. He stands up quietly.

NO. 4: Aren't you trying to make us accept a pretty incredible coincidence?

NO. 8: I'm not trying to make anyone accept it. I'm just saying it's possible.

NO. 3 *(Shouting)*: And I'm saying it's not possible.

No. 8 swiftly flicks open the blade of a switch-knife and jams it into the table next to the first one. They are exactly alike. There are several gasps and everyone stares at the knife. There is a long silence.

NO. 3 *(Slowly amazed)*: What are you trying to do?

POLICE REPORT TO PROSECUTOR

_____ POLICE DEPARTMENT   CASE NO. _____

DATE OF ARREST _____   TIME _____   A.M. P.M.

     MONTH   DAY   YEAR

ACCUSED _____   AGE _____   DATE OF BIRTH _____

   LAST   FIRST   MIDDLE   MONTH   DAY   YEAR

ADDRESS _____

   NUMBER   STREET   TOWN OR CITY   STATE

CHARGES AGAINST ACCUSED:

1. _____   PLACE OF OFFENSE: _____

                   SPECIFIC LOCATION & TOWN OR CITY

2. _____   DATE OF OFFENSE: _____ 19 _____

3. _____   HAS PREVIOUS RECORD: YES _____   NO _____

            PLACE OF ARREST: _____

                   SPECIFIC LOCATION & TOWN OR CITY

WITNESSES:

1. _____

   LAST   FIRST   MIDDLE   NUMBER   STREET   TOWN OR CITY   STATE

2. _____

   LAST   FIRST   MIDDLE   NUMBER   STREET   TOWN OR CITY   STATE

3. _____

   LAST   FIRST   MIDDLE   NUMBER   STREET   TOWN OR CITY   STATE

CIRCUMSTANCES OF ARREST (GIVE DATE AND PLACE OF OCCURRENCE, ALSO INDICATE TO WHAT WITNESS CAN TESTIFY):

_____

_____

EXHIBITS: _____

_____

_____

_____

_____

COMPANION CASE(S), IF ANY: _____

_____

_____

ARRESTING OFFICER AND IDENTIFICATION NUMBER

_____

TOWN OR CITY OF TRIAL: _____

CIRCUIT COURT NO. _____

CIRCUIT COURT

CONTINUANCES:

This report is CONFIDENTIAL and WILL NOT be available to Defense Counsel. Return to Office of Chief of Police after disposition.

CCT-45

109

"If you want a country
that's nice to live in,
you speak your voice."

STOP
PRESSION
OF
OLITIC
SSENT

7.
Dissent or
Conformity?

MR. WILLIAMS: I am a lawyer. I believe we should have respect for our laws. Many of them appear to be stupid but we, have a method whereby laws can be changed. I favor this.

MR. McGRAW: There are many more good things about America than there are bad things about America. And these radicals have had many more good things happen to them than they've had bad things. And this is not the answer to anything, really. If they have a problem, if something is wrong, and if they have a justifiable solution and they present this to adults, we would accept this and we would work with them to make this change.

SONNY FLOWERS: My family, my parents have the same values I have but, you know, I'm willing to go through the hassle to make those values real. They think changes can be made within the social structure as it is now. I don't.

TED SMITH: Too many people are getting tired of living like this. They want to change. Maybe that's what a lot of the dissent is about. Maybe, maybe they're not just protesting the war; maybe they're protesting all of society. Maybe they're protesting the life we lead right now. Their parents have brought them up, you know, well, you have to be nice, you have to go along with society. I think it's being proven right now that you don't have to. If you want a country that's nice to live in, you speak your voice.

The end cannot justify the means, for the simple and obvious reason that the means employed determine the nature of the ends produced.

—Aldous Huxley

I OCCUPY
BUILDINGS —

THROW ROCKS—

RAID FILES —

SCREAM OBSCENITIES —

AND CALL COPS PIGS —

IN AN ATTEMPT TO HUMANIZE THIS BRUTALIZED SOCIETY.

© 1969 JULES FEIFFER   5-25

I assign lots of homework—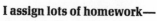

_____

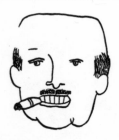 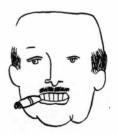

_____   _____

_____   _____

_____   _____

_____   _____

_____
_____
in an attempt to form
sensitive human beings who
can think for themselves.

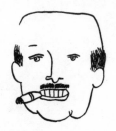 

_____
_____
in an attempt to make my son
a credit to free enterprise and
the American way of life.

_____   _____
_____   _____

ROBB CREESE: It would depend on the situation again. Sometimes the Establishment hasn't listened. And if it's necessary to start a disturbance to at least get attention in the national media, it's going to do some

What Is
The
? American ?
Way?

CHIP WILLIAMS: If a group has an idea and they feel the only way they can get it to the public is by civil disobedience, then I think they should go ahead and commit it. Because this is the land of freedom of the press, speech, religion and you should be able to show your feelings.

war is not healthy for children and other living things

LS

smoke

sit in a chair and read the newspapers.

Millions of men go to war, acres of them are
buried, guns and ships broken, cities
burned, villages sent up in smoke,
and children where cows are killed off
amid hoarse barbecues vanish like
finger-rings of smoke in a north wind.

sit in a chair and read the newspapers.

—CARL SANDBURG

It is sweet and honorab

We're here because
We're here because
We're here because
We're here;
We're here because
We're here because
We're here because
We're here . . .

> *Marching song of the British Expeditionary Force, France, 1917, sung to the tune of "Auld Lang Syne."*

Soldiers who wish to be a hero
Are practically zero,
But those who wish to be civilians,
Jesus, they run into the millions

> *G.I. scribbling on latrine wall in England, WW II.*

Older men declare war. But it

die for one's country.
—Horace

Last night I had the strangest dream
I ever had before
I dreamed the world had all agreed
To put an end to war ...

... Call it peace
Or call it treason,
Call it love
Or call it reason,
But I ain't marchin' any more ...

uth that must fight and die.
—Herbert Hoover

HOOKS AND SHELLS   **BY BEN GARRIS**

Give Thanks For Patriotic Youths

For ten long years we have watched with disgust and considerable misgiving the downgrading of patriotism in this country. First, the "beat generation," as they aptly termed themselves, talked of placing self above country.

Then came the hippies, wallowing in filth and self love, who spat upon the flag and called it "doing their thing."

Next were the "students," less their ignorant, yellow little souls, who mouthed four letter words at any square who spoke well of God or Country. They gathered themselves together in motley little crews called "SDS," and cursed the "Establishment," which paid for their food, clothes, schools, and foolishness.

Colleges were taken over, and the gutless members of the faculty joined the whines against ROTC and any research which the students didn't like or didn't understand.

Somewhere along the line, colleges had neglected to impart to the students the simple fact that it is the armed services of his country which have guaranteed all the freedoms which the students now abuse. Perhaps the professors have not imparted this because they do not understand it themselves.

The wire service stories in the daily papers and the articles in national news magazines devoted their space to meticulous, blow by blow descriptions of flag burnings, draft board burglaries, troop train protests, and defense contractor harassment. They have avoided the word "patriotism" like the plague, but they have not hesitated to take the protestors' side against the hard-pressed police and soldiers.

Remember, during past wars, returning troops were greeted by cheering throngs, who grinned and threw kisses? Now, returning troops are greeted by jeering throngs who grimace and throw bricks.

Patriotism is out and "protesting" is the "in" thing.

But, thank God, not everywhere—yet.

First Enlistment Figures: U.S. Department of Defense

Fiscal Year	Army	Navy	Marines	Air Force	Total
1965	101,901	94,301	34,310	87,697	318,20
1966	170,113	143,144	68,856	166,122	548,23
1967	190,320	101,083	71,289	120,781	483,47
1968	198,860	122,793	93,013	98,422	513,08
1969	200,755	147,085	83,619	123,314	554,77

WHAT'S IT LIKE

TO BECOME A MARINE ?

Building the Marine Corps team is very much like building a winning team on the athletic field.

First, the volunteers selected are proud, and capable. They are able to meet high mental and physical standards.

Second, they expect to train and to train hard, developing new muscle, sharpening reflexes and improving their mental abilities.

Third, they work as a team, yet are prepared to lead as individuals.

Finally, they wear a uniform and carry an emblem of which they are proud.

When you join the Marines you become a member of a team which, in nearly 200 years of eventful service, has never met defeat.

The Marine Corps

BUILDS MEN

SEE YOUR MARINE RECRUITER

NAVMC 6710   GPO : 1961 O - 578955

CONGRESSIONAL

Monday, December 11, 1967

Mr. EDWARDS of Louisiana. Mr. Speaker, BILL STUCKEY could not be called middle aged at 32. Although his votes on the social security legislation and his own proposal to raise outside earning levels for senior citizens clearly show that Congressman STUCKEY is aware of and concerned with the senior citizens of his district, he has not neglected the young people, that group of people who will be the leaders and decisionmakers of our country in just a few years.

On several occasions the gentleman from Georgia [Mr. STUCKEY] has spoken out in defense of the youth of Georgia and the Eighth District, praising their responsibility and contrasting them to the irresponsible "hippies" that made headlines all last summer and I commend him for so doing. He said recently:

While the streets of Georgetown in Washington and Haight-Ashbury in San Francisco and Greenwich Village in New York were filled with mobs of so-called "hippies" and "teenie-boppers" wandering aimlessly about, conducting sit-in's, lie-in's, and wed-in's, we had no such irresponsible conduct in our District. And, neither did any of our young people travel to these other cities to take part.

Congressman STUCKEY said that while the activities of these "hippies" made every major magazine in the country, no such coverage was given to the outstanding achievements of our young people of the Eighth District or others just like them across the country who spent their summer working at summer jobs to help earn their own spending money or money to further their educations and who spent their summer participating in constructive activities.

RECORD

In a speech praising the accomplishments of the members of the Valdosta High School Band and the Waycross Band, Congressman STUCKEY said:

Full length stories, complete with pictures were written about those unclean individuals who openly used a chemical drug called LSD and who smoked marijuana, commonly referred to as "pot" or "grass". Meanwhile the Valdosta High School Band, made up of a fine group of clean, wholesome young people, worked together as a team and won first place in the Cherry Blossom Festival Band Competition in Washington last spring.

And just a few weeks ago, the Waycross High School Band was selected over many other bands throughout the country to perform before 50,000 spectators at the Washington Redskins Football game in Washington.

The gentleman from Georgia [Mr. STUCKEY] says that he believes that the experience our young people receive from such activities participated in by these two bands from Valdosta and Waycross is extremely valuable. He has said:

These young people learn how to work together as a team. They learn to respect their fellow students. And, they become aware of the fact their individual effort mean the success of the entire group.

Congressman STUCKEY commended the young people of the Eighth District and gave special recognition to the members of the two bands for their outstanding achievements.

Ryniker, Margaret   June, 1968
Masonic Lodge Essay Contest   Bath, New York

ARE THE ACCOMPLISHMENTS
OF OUR YOUTH NEWSWORTHY?

"Vandalism on the Rise," "Teenagers
Arrested at Drug Party," "Juvenile Delin-
quents Steal Lincoln Memorial." Do these
headlines look vaguely familiar? In almost
every newspaper or magazine you pick up there
is at least one article on the "wild youth of
today." However, don't forget the headlines
that are side by side with these—"Respected
Banker Steals $50,000" or "56 year old Man
Shoots Wife and 5 Children." So be it of adult
or youth a story to be newsworthy has to
concern murder or mayhem or disaster. The
achievements and worthwhile accomplishments
do not make good copy and would not sell many
newspapers, but let's list a few. The Student
Exchange Programs, UNICEF, Red Cross and
March of Dimes crusades, students raising
money to build school in some remote part of
the world, hospital volunteers, or Project
Headstart. These things are not even published in the want ads!

How about looking back to the "Roaring
Twenties" with it's flaming youth and
flappers and rolled stockings and rumble
seats? Most of them grew up to be solid citizens, not all, but this is not Utopia.
I found a quotation that interested me
greatly on this point. "What is happening to
our youth? They are wild and unruly and have
lost respect for parents and for home. There
is far too much drinking and carousing."—

Do you know who said that? Billy Graham or Bishop Sheen? No, Aristotle said it centuries ago in the days of the Glorious Greek Civilization. So in answer to my title, yes, we do have many noteworthy accomplishments. Someday they will be remembered and then we will be the adult world and there will be a different younger generation for us to turn our thoughts to.

For the present we ask that you look for the good in us because it really is there. We're not all perfect examples of do-gooders, but don't give up all hope. We have many fine newsworthy accomplishments to our credit and given a chance we will have many more. Look back and remember what our grandparents thought about you as your generation was growing up. Well, you turned out to be pretty good citizens and with luck and the help of the Lord so will we.

OFFICE OF ECONOMIC OPPORTUNITY
VISTA VOLUNTEER APPLICATION

Card #71 (1, 2)

SOCIAL SECURITY NO. 3-11

Form Approved, Budget Bureau No. 116-R0016

SECTION I - ESSENTIAL INFORMATION

NOTE: VISTA Assignments Require Difficult or Unusual Living Conditions. PLEASE Keep This In Mind When Filling Out This Application.
(Print or use a typewriter, and answer all questions.)

a. LAST NAME (MR.) (MRS.) (MISS)

12-24 FIRST NAME   25-34 MIDDLE OR MAIDEN   35

b. SEX   36

c. HEIGHT   d. WEIGHT

e. DATE OF BIRTH
MONTH 37-38   DAY 39-40   YEAR 41-42

f. PLACE OF BIRTH *(City, state, country)*

g. AVAILABILITY FOR VISTA SERVICE *(Notify VISTA immediately if this date changes.)*
I will be available for VISTA service ⟶   MONTH 43-44   DAY 45-46   YEAR

SECTION II - WORK ASSIGNMENTS *(Continued)*

NO CARD

b. WORK ASSIGNMENT PREFERENCE

Many different VISTA assignments are possible. Please check columns as applicable, listed below.

LINE CODE	TYPE OF ASSIGNMENT	WOULD NOT ACCEPT	LINE CODE	TYPE OF ASSIGNMENT	WOULD NOT ACCEPT
1.	Work with non-English speaking people.		10.	Work with the physically handicapped.	
2.	Work with homemakers.		11.	Work with elderly people.	
3.	Work as a recreation leader.		12.	Work with mentally ill.	
4.	Work with law, crime or delinquency.		13.	Work in community health centers.	
5.	Work with pre-school children.		14.	Work independently.	
6.	Work with grade school children.		15.	Work as a member of a team of Volunteers.	
7.	Work with teen-age groups; tutoring, recreation, counseling.		16.	Work with small groups, i.e., town counsels, planning groups.	
8.	Work with the mentally retarded.		17.	Work in an education capacity, basic, remedial, special.	
9.	Work in a social agency or settlement house.		18.		

General Skill Areas are listed below. In Section "a.", please check one column for EVERY skill listed. In Section "b.", mark only ONE of these skills for your best skill. Mark only one of the skills for your second best skill. Mark only one of these skills for your third best skill.

147-58

a. GENERAL SKILL AREA	HIGHLY SKILLED	SOME SKILL	NONE	b. EXTENT OF SKILL
1. HEALTH, MEDICINE, NURSING, AND RELATED FIELDS (Specify)				LIST BEST SKILL ___ 47-49
2. MUSIC, ARTS, DRAMA				
3. RECREATION OR ATHLETICS				HOW DID YOU LEARN THIS SKILL? ___ 50
4. CRAFTS				
5. BUSINESS, SALES, RETAIL TRADES				HOW LONG HAVE YOU PRACTICED THIS SKILL?
6. CLERICAL OR SECRETARIAL				DATES: FROM ___ TO ___
7. SCIENCE, SOCIAL, GROUP WORK				LIST SECOND BEST SKILL ___ 51-53
8. SCIENCE, PHYSICAL OR BIOLOGICAL				
9. TEACHING, TUTORING				HOW DID YOU LEARN THIS SKILL? ___ 54
10. HOME ECONOMICS (Specify)				
11. LAW				HOW LONG HAVE YOU PRACTICED THIS SKILL?
12. ENGINEERING (Specify)				DATES: FROM ___ TO ___
13. AGRICULTURE AND RELATED FIELDS (Specify)				LIST THIRD BEST SKILL /Special Skill ___ 55-57
14. CONSTRUCTION AND INDUSTRIAL: MASON, CARPENTER, ELECTRICIAN, PLUMBER, MECHANIC, ETC. (Specify)				
15. GENERAL LABORER (Specify)				

SECTION XIV - In the following space, explain why you would like to be a VISTA Volunteer. (If you use additional paper, be sure to include your name and Application No. See Page 2, Item R, for Application No.)

SONNY FLOWERS: I hate. What I hate is something else again. I don't hate whites. I don't hate yellow people. I don't hate a group of people. I hate a thing. I hate oppression and I hate exploitation, you know. I hate racism.

his agitation. "Yeah! Yeah! But who's going to do the pushing?" he quipped.

Everyone began to talk at once to fill in the yawning pit of probability.

"I'm not afraid," said Claudia. "I mean I think I'm not afraid."

"Those pickets don't worry me a bit," Robby said coldly, evenly. "All I want is some day to get the chance to tell those kids in Fayette, 'Buddy boy, I don't go for you any more than you go for me. You just let me get what's mine, and we'll call it quits.' "

"That's the wrong attitude," Joyce protested hotly. "You've got to start out feeling you can be friends."

A howl of derision came from Amos. "Sure thing, ask your new white friends to drop in and have some chitlings with you," he mimicked in a falsetto, "and see what happens."

"Just the same, it's the wrong way to start out," Joyce insisted. "You won't get them to like you that way."

The talk stopped abruptly as Main Street came into view. Robby halted, and before Linda realized what he wanted, he grabbed her hand and was saying to the others, "Get in line." They formed a column, and Amos and Jerry fell in place protectively behind the four paired girls.

It was a small, silent column. As the distance between him and Fayette began to shorten, Robby could see people near the school. He remembered that in the old days (in that dim past) when the bus took him to Carver, he used to pass Fayette and see the white kids in front of the school. He wondered fleetingly now if he could make out the sheep from the lions.

Even before he had time to abandon that vain effort, he heard a voice cry out wildly, "Here come the niggers!" His scalp prickled as he became aware of the blur of white placards waving crazily in the air. The distance between him and the cement path which he would have to walk to get to the school doors was getting very short, but his mind had shut tight against reading the pickets' signs. He heard the cry:

NATURE IS THE PAIN OF A NEW IDEA.

—Walter Bagehot

YOU THE READER

Face to Face

with an actively political antipollutionist

"Last summer some of the local beaches were closed down. They weren't safe for swimming anymore; the municipal waste plant had been dumping sewage into the water," says Mike Sweeney, seventeen, of Deerfield, Illinois. Many of his neighbors reacted with anger, with rage—but not Mike. "I don't get enraged about anything. It's bad politics. Angry, emotional people are an easy threat to deal with—a few soothing words and they'll calm down and go home. The only way to solve the pollution problem is with rational discussion and a tremendous amount of carefully applied political persuasion and pressure."

Mike, who was appointed late last year to the United States Department of the Interior's youth advisory group, SCOPE (Student Council on Pollution and the Environment), calmly took a look around him and decided it was just "a matter of priorities." "We have a lot of problems in this country, but I felt that pollution was the most urgent. If something isn't done about it soon, we're in trouble. In about twenty years from now every major lake in the country will be closed. Whole species of plants and animals will die off. Hundreds of people will die every time a mass of stagnant air settles over a city. And we'll eventually have to find a substitute for water."

Mike was originally drawn into the fight against pollution by the principal of his school, Deerfield High. "Mr. Retsholdt was very interested in the problem and asked me, as president of the student council, to help. I called a meeting of students and parents, and we started writing letters to *anybody* who could do something—senators, state legislators, local officials, the President, the Secretary of the Interior." Mike's letters were pragmatic and to the point. "I told them that anyone could say he's against pollution. Who's for it? But the real measure of a man, of a politician, is whether he votes for appropriations to implement the battle." Mike firmly believes that young people all over the country can help win the battle of the environment by joining antipollution groups—and by writing letters. "If you sound reasonably intelligent, the person you're writing to won't know how young you are. Just let the man know that if he doesn't vote for funds to help clean up the air and water, *you* won't vote for him in the next election. That's kind of sneaky, but necessary—unless you want to walk around with air tanks on your back thirty years from now."

"*Well—how about it, Dad?*"

8.
Generation
Gap?

A LETTER FROM A SKEPTICAL SON TO HIS BALD-HEADED DAD

Dear Dad:

Last time I was home, you said some significant things about my interest in radical proposals for a new social order. When you told me I was too young for sane opinion on such matters, you insinuated that your generation is better qualified to find "the way out" than mine. I question this assumption. I do not believe that those who led us into this mess are capable of "leading" us out.

Dad, believe me when I say that I am indebted to you for paternal love and protection, but believe me also when I say that my generation holds in contempt the colossal social, economic, and political blunders which you perpetuated. As we survey the worthless heritage of crime, war, poverty and greed, we unite in shouting, "We will have none of it. There must be a second Renaissance!" And we scrutinize our entire inheritance to find the true value of these institutions. If you say our sin is lack of respect, then we can answer, "Veneration was your sin."

"Our capitalistic democracy is the ultimate in modern government," I have heard you brag. May I call your attention to the metropolitan editor who recently said "I support this man because he is the least crooked of the three." "Trust our economic leaders," you assure me.

I answer, "Men are starving today in the shadows of your rotting granaries and hog-butchering establishments, Dad. Under your system privation increases in proportion to the increase in production. "Hold fast to the religion of your fathers" you warn, and I cannot help wondering, "Has that religion lessened hatred, crime, war and suffering in its 20-century trial? Are its fundamental concepts philosophically sound?"

Dad, our young people are admittedly a skeptical crowd. What we have lost in the comfort of blind faith, we have gained in the assurance of empirical, scientific reasoning. If this fact-facing attitude be heresy, you may style us "heretics." If we worship reality instead of sublimity, you may say that we are fools. If science has altered our moral convictions, and if our new freedom conflicts with your age-old prohibitions, then you may consign us to your fiery hells.

But: One thing is certain. Win or lose, right or wrong, we are beginning to THINK THROUGH these things. We are trying to see "beyond our noses"; we are striving to build a better world . . . In that struggle we ask your cooperation, realizing that our youthful ambition, coupled with your aged perspective, is the one combination which can solve the riddle of these times.

Well—how about it, Dad?

The above editorial appeared in the KENT STATER campus newspaper in 1934. It was written by the student editor, Walter W. Seifert, now an associate professor of journalism at OSU. Today, at 55, he is a confessed conservative, "A sort of middle-of-the-roader—halfway between Barry Goldwater and the John Birch Society." He says, regarding the quoted editorial, "The more things change, the more they stay the same. This editorial could have been written by any of our young rebels just yesterday."

The child is father of the man. —**William Wordsworth**

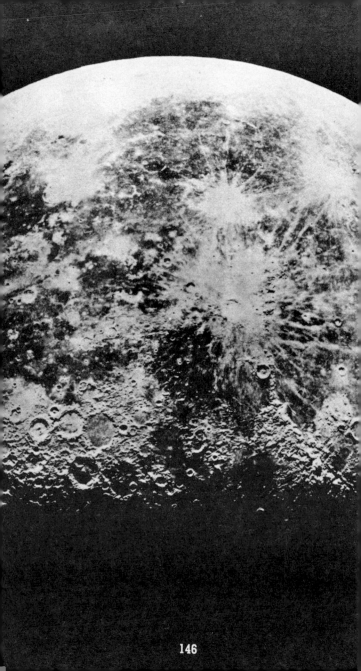

archives

generation upon
generation upon
generation upon
generation upon
generation upon
generation upon
generation upon
generation upon
generation upon
generation upon
generation upon
generation upon
generation upon
generation upon
generation upon
generation upon
generation upon
generation upon
generation upon
g neration upon
g neration up n
g nerat on up n
g nerat n up n
g nerat n p n
g erat   n p n
g era   n p n
g era   n   n
g er   n   n
g   r   n   n
g   n   n
g   n
g

A complete teacher's guide to DIG/U.S.A. may be obtained by writing to
Bantam Books, Inc.
School and College Division
666 Fifth Avenue
New York, New York 10019

Individual and Group Summary Projects

1. Write a well-documented article expressing your view of today's youth. You may choose one particular aspect of today's youth (morality, drugs, appearance, political activity, etc.)

2. Prepare a questionnaire to be administered to thirty or more adults and/or students which explores attitudes toward some phase of youth or adult behavior. Report the results to your class.

3. Prepare an annotated bibliography of twenty-five books and magazine articles on youth appropriate for your class.

4. Prepare a series of six charts and graphs which reflect certain confirmed data about young people, i.e., on crime, education; morality, residence, opinions, interests, etc.

5. Read the six books excerpted in the text (*Manchild in The Promised Land, I'm Really Dragged But Nothing Gets Me Down, The House of Tomorrow, Escape from Nowhere, Two Blocks Apart,* and *Lions in The Way.*) Report to your class the special dilemmas and experiences of the young people portrayed.

6. Write a letter to a congressman, a newspaper editor, a TV station, and to a community or national organization concerning their treatment of issues of interest to youth or concerning their publicly expressed attitudes about youth.

7. Collect, duplicate, and distribute to the class the lyrics from ten popular songs which deal with the problems of youth. Play some of the recordings for the class. Be prepared to help the class interpret difficult passages.

8. Make a photomontage of *your* youth from pictures of the people, places, events, things, etc. that were and are important to you.

9. Collect, duplicate, and distribute to the class 10 poems about youth and age, or youth and war, or about being young. Prepare to describe to the class similar and contrasting ideas in the poems you collected and the special means used to convey them.

10. Prepare a reading of a poem having special interest for young people. Accompany your reading with appropriate music, sound, and visual effects (lights, slides, props).

11. Make an 8mm film study of an activity as performed by a young person and by an adult. Emphasize either the difference or similarity of the performances. Appropriate activities: eating, putting on makeup, combing hair, dancing, talking on the telephone . . . etc.

12. Make an 8mm film portrait of a young man or young woman, an adult, a member of your family.

13. Tape-record the special sounds of a generation: rock music, jangling phone, motorcycle, teenage conversation . . . etc., typewriters, commuter train, bridge club, organization meeting, factory noises, turning pages of a newspaper . . . etc.

14. Read five of the following plays: *Our Town, Look Homeward, Angel, A Thousand Clowns, Raisin in the Sun, Take a Giant Step, Ah, Wilderness, West Side Story, Bye, Bye Birdie.* Report on the relationships between the young and adult characters, their similar and differing aspirations, their fears, the roles each plays in affecting the lives of the others. With the help of other students, tape-record key scenes, play them for your class, and explain why they are particularly significant.

15. Over a two-week period collect and catalog every youth-involved news story, editorial, article, cartoon, survey, chart, or advertisement appearing in one newspaper.

16. Make a study of a magazine published for young people. Describe the features, advertisements, pictures, tone, special appeals, typical stories or articles, kinds of people who read it (suggested by all of these items and by letters to the editors).

17. Review five films in which the problems of young people provide the major focus. What are their problems? Who or what is responsible for them? How do they contend with these problems and with what results? Describe similarities and differences in problems treated among the five films. Note, too, similarities and differences in the styles, behavior, attitudes, morality of the young protagonists.

18. Using a tape recorder, interview your parents or some adult about their attitudes toward some of the issues raised in the book.

19. List the leisure-time activities of young people in your community. Indicate pleasures and dangers inherent in such activities and parental attitudes toward the ways in which youth fills its leisure time. Suggest additional recreational possibilities.

20. Tape-record the speech of young people in varying contexts: school, home, ball-field, social event. Describe the differences and similarities in the kinds of words used, and the way words are put together to form sentences. Do the same for adults, recording their speech at home, at work, and at a social event.

21. a. Make a list and explain the origins of twenty-five teen-age slang terms.

   b. Make a list and explain the origins of fifteen words commonly used by the general population which originated in the teenage world.

   c. Prepare a glossary (See p. 59) of at least twenty-five special words or phrases used in one of the following: sports, rock-pop scene, drugs, cars and motorcycles, school, appearance, fashion.

22. Tape-record the speech of five students having marked differences in their dialects. Contrast each dialect with what is standard in your community, noting specific vowel and consonant sound differences, unusual rising and falling pitches, special stress of particular sounds, and the use of unusual words or phrases.

23. Do a comparative study of driver's license and auto insurance regulations in at least ten states in your general region. Include an account of restrictions on motorcycle use.

24. Form a committee to arrange for an assembly program which features students and adults who will discuss any one or several issues about young people and adults raised in this book.

25. Make a bulletin board display matching pictures from newspapers and magazines with appropriate quotations.

26. Choose a subject suggested by the book (generation gap, drugs, teenage crime, the various activities of youth), and make a collage.

27. Collect at least twenty artifacts and documents which you feel should have been included in the book and prepare appropriate questions, quotations and activities for each.

Inventory

SECTION 2—THE FAMILY

SECTION 3—LIFE STYLES

SECTION 4—A NEW MORALITY?

SECTION 5—DRUGS

SECTION 6—CRIME

SECTION 7—DISSENT OR CONFORMITY?

SECTION 8—GENERATION GAP?

INDIVIDUAL AND GROUP SUMMARY PROJECTS

ACKNOWLEDGMENTS

Graffito: "Love," etc. appearing on Inside Covers: From *Graffiti U.S.A.* Copyright © 1967 by Alexicon Corporation. Reprinted by permission of Kanrom, Inc. and WNEW–FM, New York.

Excerpt from *The Prophet* by Kahlil Gibran. Copyright 1923 by Kahlil Gibran; renewed 1951 by the Administrators C.T.A. of Kahlil Gibran Estate and Mary G. Gibran. Reprinted by permission of Alfred A. Knopf, Inc.

Photo of college student on page 8. From *Northeastern News*, August 22, 1969. Copyright © 1969 by *Northeastern News* and reprinted with their permission.

"The Generation Gap," from *The Hartford Times*, September 9, 1969. Copyright © 1969 by *The Hartford Times* and reprinted with their permission.

Ten small pictures of youths and adults on pages 15–17 by Suleiman D. Zalatimo. Reprinted by permission of Suleiman D. Zalatimo.

Lyrics from "My Generation," by Peter Townshend. Copyright © 1965 by Fabulous Music, Ltd., London. All publication rights controlled by TRO–Devon Music, Inc., New York, for North America. International Copyright Secured. All Rights Reserved Including Public Performance For Profit. Reprinted by permission of TRO–Devon Music, Inc.

"The Small Society," by Brickman, September 28, 1969. Copyright © 1969 by King Features Syndicate, Inc. and reprinted with their permission.

Chart and table from Data on Youth by the New York State Division for Youth. Reprinted by permission of New York State Division for Youth.

"The Family," by P. Marisol. Reprinted by permission of The Museum of Modern Art.

Excerpts from Ann Landers' Columns appearing in *The Hartford Courant*, on pages 26, 69. Copyright © 1969 by Ann Landers. Reprinted by permission of Publishers-Hall Syndicate.

"Runaway Ads," from *The Village Voice*. Copyright © 1969 by The Village Voice, Inc. and reprinted with their permission.

Excerpts from *The Nations Youth*, Children's Bureau Publication 460, on pages 28–29, 66–67, 93, 96–97. Reprinted by permission of Department of Health, Education and Welfare, Office of Child Development.

Excerpt from *Two Blocks Apart* edited by Charlotte Leon Mayerson. Copyright © 1965 by Holt, Rinehart & Winston, Inc. and reprinted with their permission.

Telephone Advertisement. Reprinted by permission of American Telephone and Telegraph Company, Long Lines Department.

"Mother to Son," by Langston Hughes. From his *Selected Poems*. Copyright 1926 by Alfred A. Knopf, Inc., renewed 1954 by Langston Hughes. Reprinted by permission of Alfred A. Knopf, Inc.

Excerpt from *Manchild in the Promised Land* by Claude Brown. Copyright © 1965 by Claude Brown. Reprinted by permission of The Macmillan Company.

Excerpt from '*I'm Really Dragged Out But Nothing Gets Me Down,*' by Nat Hentoff. Copyright © 1968 by Namar Publications, Ltd. and reprinted with their permission and that of Simon & Schuster, Inc.

Article from *Advertising Age*, March 10, 1969. Copyright © 1970 by Crain Communications, Inc. Reprinted by permission of Advertising Age.

"Mom and Dad," by Frank Zappa. From his *We're Only In It For the Money*. Copyright © 1968 by Frank Zappa Music, Inc. and reprinted with their permission.

GOD ISN'T DEAD—
HE JUST DOESN'T
TO GET INVOLVED

G

CHICKEN
LITTLE
WAS
RIGHT